THE *New* TRADITIONAL WOODWORKER

From Tool Set to Skill Set to Mind Set

JIM TOLPIN

POPULAR WOODWORKING BOOKS
CINCINNATI, OHIO
www.popularwoodworking.com

Read This Important Safety Notice

To prevent accidents, keep safety in mind while you work. Use the safety guards installed on power equipment; they are for your protection.

When working on power equipment, keep fingers away from saw blades, wear safety goggles to prevent injuries from flying wood chips and sawdust, wear hearing protection and consider installing a dust vacuum to reduce the amount of airborne sawdust in your woodshop.

Don't wear loose clothing, such as neckties or shirts with loose sleeves, or jewelry, such as rings, necklaces or bracelets, when working on power equipment. Tie back long hair to prevent it from getting caught in your equipment.

People who are sensitive to certain chemicals should check the chemical content of any product before using it.

Due to the variability of local conditions, construction materials, skill levels, etc., neither the author nor Popular Woodworking Books assumes any responsibility for any accidents, injuries, damages or other losses incurred resulting from the material presented in this book.

The authors and editors who compiled this book have tried to make the contents as accurate and correct as possible. Plans, illustrations, photographs and text have been carefully checked. All instructions, plans and projects should be carefully read, studied and understood before beginning construction.

Prices listed for supplies and equipment were current at the time of publication and are subject to change.

Metric Conversion Chart

TO CONVERT	TO	MULTIPLY BY
Inches	Centimeters	2.54
Centimeters	Inches	0.4
Feet	Centimeters	30.5
Centimeters	Feet	0.03
Yards	Meters	0.9
Meters	Yards	1.1

Distributed in Canada by Fraser Direct
100 Armstrong Avenue
Georgetown, Ontario L7G 5S4
Canada

Distributed in the U.K. and Europe by F+W Media International
Brunel House
Newton Abbot
Devon TQ12 4PU
England
Tel: (+44) 1626 323200
Fax: (+44) 1626 323319
E-mail: postmaster@davidandcharles.co.uk

Distributed in Australia by Capricorn Link
P.O. Box 704
Windsor, NSW 2756
Australia

Visit our Web site at www.popularwoodworking.com.

Other fine Popular Woodworking Books are available from your local bookstore or direct from the publisher.

ACQUISITIONS EDITOR: David Thiel
DESIGNER: Brian Roeth
PRODUCTION COORDINATOR: Mark Griffin
PHOTOGRAPHER: Craig Wester
ILLUSTRATOR: JIM TOLPIN

About the Author

Over the last three decades, Jim has worked professionally in woodworking as a boatbuilder, a timber-frame housewright, and a custom cabinetmaker. He has also authored books and articles about general woodworking, cabinetmaking and finish carpentry — and more recently about home design. His how-to articles have been published in most of the major woodworking magazines including, *Fine Woodworking, Popular Woodworking Magazine* and *Fine Homebuilding*. He writes regular columns for *CabinetMaker* and *Woodshop News* magazines and has written a number of feature articles for *Cottage* and *Coastal Living* magazines. He has also produced twelve books in this period of time that have together sold more than 750,000 copies to date. Jim is the immediate past president of a technical writer's trade organization: The National Association for Home and Workshop Writers. He is one of the founders and faculty members of the Port Townsend School of Woodworking.

Acknowledgements

John Marckworth and Tim Lawson (my fellow teachers and founders of the Port Townsend School of Woodworking).

Christine Hemp for insightful and incisive editing during the early stages of the manuscript.

Garrett Hack, Ole Kanestrom, Greg Kossow, Steve Habersetzer, Dan Packard, Nolle Pritchard, Mila Polina, Mike Wenzloff and Jacob Middleton for encouragement and for actually sharing tricks of the hand tool trade with me during the course of writing this book.

Craig Wester for his, once again, expert photography.

Yuri Tolpin for contributing to the graphic design of some of the images.

Chris Schwarz for the gut check of where I was going with this book.

Hats off to the production folks at F+W including my editor David Thiel, and designer Brian Roeth.

And, on the home front, my wife Cathy and mini-shop mate Abel.

CONTENTS

FOREWORD

I didn't think I would need to write another book on woodworking. I figured the ten other books I wrote on the subject pretty much covered it — at least from my point of view as a professional cabinetmaker and finish carpenter. However, in the last few years I've turned from tradework to teaching hand tool woodworking. Many of my students encouraged me to write yet another book because they couldn't find a one that showed them what I was teaching.

These students (most of whom were new to woodworking), wanted to learn to make solid wood furniture and small furnishings for themselves in a modest-sized, home workshop. They weren't all drawn to my hand tool courses because they had some particular fascination with hand tools or were fans of traditional woodworking. Instead, many were reluctant to deal with the inherent noise, dust and danger of power tools as well as the large space and investment demanded by them.

When I stepped into their shoes I could see their dilemma: There wasn't a single, comprehensive book that would show them how to set up and outfit a primarily hand-tool workshop, and then show how to use these human-powered tools in the most efficient ways. They certainly weren't going to find these things out from most woodworking and home improvement shows on television. Tool aisles at big box stores wouldn't help, nor would their memories of high school shop (it was

"Just because people are dead, doesn't mean they were stupid!"

— ANON

*"What the machine does by brute force,
you will be able to do with quiet cunning"*
— JOHN BROWN, WELSH CHAIRMAKER

called "Industrial Arts" for a reason!) These sources point people toward working with wood as a medium to be machined. In this mindset, tools and techniques are presented in a way that mimic the tooling and processing strategies of the industrial, production furniture maker and not those of the pre-industrial artisan. It turns out, my students have much more in common with the latter. The bottom line was that these folks wanted to learn to work wood rather than to *machine* wood because they wanted to make things rather than *manufacture* things.

So my students didn't really need to learn how to use routers, power sanders, biscuit joiners, chopsaws or even a table saw to build furniture. They also don't need to deal with plywood, toxic finishes or make arithmetic calculations and develop cutlists in order to make one-off pieces of furniture by hand.

So they were right: I did need to write another book. I needed to show them that building furniture with hand tools — while certainly taking longer than it might in a shop filled with machinery — is not that difficult to learn or tedious to do. In fact, they would discover that working wood by hand can, and should be, quite pleasurable. The book would thoroughly cover such fundamentals as how to lay out and equip a hand tool shop to make it an efficient and pleasant place in which to work; how to identify hand-tool friendly wood; and how to choose and use the most appropriate hand tool for the work at hand.

This, I hope, is the book they asked me to write.

JIM TOLPIN | PORT TOWNSEND, WA | MARCH 18, 2010

INTRODUCTION

Born Again in Hand Tool Heaven

Who, exactly, is the "New Traditional" woodworker? Well, it may be you if you are as interested in wood and the process of working it as you are in the products that you can make from it. It may be you if you are fascinated by the idea of taking a tool in hand and immersing yourself in a quietly challenging and fully engrossing process rather than working at a machine to arrive at an outcome as quickly as possible. But it may not be you if you are thinking of making a living at woodworking with hand tools! Instead, New Traditional Woodworking is about doing woodworking with the goal of feeling the texture of the wood; of smelling its aroma; and of hearing the crisp "snick" of your handplane as you stroke the tool across a board.

Now, I am not advocating that the new traditional woodworker totally abstain from using power tools. Just as pre-industrial furniture makers bought their stock pre-cut to thickness from a sawyer, I think we should too. (Though, in our case, we're more likely to shop at a hardwood lumberyard than at a sawyer's mill yard). I also expect that you will true — or have someone else true — the majority of your boards flat and to within 1/16" of finished thickness with a surface planer. You may also choose, as I did, to use these two relatively safe and quiet power tools to ease the work: A band saw to rip long lengths of stock, resaw boards to thickness and to occasionally cut long curves; and a drill press to remove most of the waste in larger mortises and to drill critical alignment and fastening holes. The bottom line here is that New Traditional Woodworking is not about going back in time to

A proud student at the Port Townsend School of Woodworking shows off his first all-handtool project.

endure a tedious vocation. Instead, it is about immersing oneself in a pleasurable avocation.

So here's what I think you'll enjoy doing with hand tools:
- Cutting and trimming pieces to exact width and length
- Cutting joints such as dovetails and mortise and tenons
- Making dadoes and rabbets
- Shaping and smoothing the wood to a ready-to-finish surface
- Making rounded and molded edges

The reality is, for one-off, non-production furniture pieces, handwork doesn't add a significant amount of time. Some hand processes such as cutting compound angles, shaping edges to a profile and smoothing surfaces to a mirror finish actually go much faster with hand tools than they take with machines (especially when you include set up time). Contrary to what you've likely seen on television, you really don't need a table saw, a chopsaw, a power sander or a router!

If you set up your shop and build the fixtures that I present in this book, then welcome to Hand Tool Heaven! Here you will experience the true joy of woodworking that comes through using hand tools and the power of your own body to work the wood. With practice you will soon gain:

• …an intimate relationship with wood: Based on my experiences in the nearly 40 years I've been doing woodworking, I've found that the more power you apply to the process, the further you get from the product. In working wood by hand you cut and shape the parts with the power of your muscles, the guidance of your eyes and the feel of your hands — and that means you get to know intimately every piece of wood in your project. Remember, you are working wood, not machining wood.

A smoothing plane, properly tuned and sharpened, produces a smoother surface than can any amount of power sanding.

• …the ability to do advanced woodworking with a high degree of safety: While hand tools such as chisels can be dangerous (as a kitchen knife can be dangerous), safe handling techniques can be quickly learned that keep these tools well under control. Also, hand tools are inherently quiet and do not produce toxic dust — just shavings. (In contrast, the fine dust produced by power sanders and other woodworking machines is carcinogenic and, at the least, can aggravate allergies). So while working with hand tools, you will not have to spend the day wearing gear to protect your ears, eyes and lungs to work safely.

• …an affordable hobby. A set of basic, but adequate, hand tools costs much less than the power tools you would need to do the same tasks. Many affordable, yet high quality hand tools (vintage, pre-WWII hand tools are usually the best bet) can be found at yard sales and flea markets — or through internet auction sites or dealer's websites. Hand tool woodworking also requires far less space than a power tool-primary shop and doesn't (obviously) require special wiring for heavy power tools or plumbing systems for dust collection.

• …a quickly increasing ability to achieve mastery with the tools. Unlike a table saw or power jointer which require you to climb a steep,

intense learning curve in order to use them safely and properly, you can learn to use hand tools safely, efficiently and accurately surprising quickly. The secret is that there is no special secret to using them. It's just a matter of being shown the proper way to set up and handle these tools and to then practice the techniques until you've locked them into muscle memory. I regularly teach sharpening plane blades and chisels to a razor edge in a one-day class. I can teach raw beginners to cut joints and plane edges and surfaces with amazing accuracy within a one-week hand tool course. Just as in learning to dance or speak another language, as you master one tool mastering another tends to come more quickly.

• …the pleasure of other people's company: When you work primarily with hand tools you aren't insulated from the environment or from the pleasure of other people's company. You are free from wearing dust masks, face shields, hearing protection and from the exposure of people to machines that can turn wood into lethal projectiles. If you limit finishing to the lovely aroma and long-lasting sheen of non-toxic beeswax and oil products, then odors aren't an issue either. This means you can work freely around other people, including children and pets. In fact, you can — and I often do — include them! My five-year-old son learned in less than ten minutes how to cut dowels accurately to length using a backsaw and a bench hook. The dog, however, took a little longer…

Before the next section of the book, however, I want to be sure that the following, most-commonly-asked questions have been answered:

Isn't handwork difficult? (Don't hand tools work slowly and take a lot of strength to use?)

In most people's prior experiences, the answer would be yes: They were slow, they were not that precise, and they took a lot of strength. It is also true, however, that most people have never had the experience of using a hand tool that has been tuned and sharpened to its full potential and then given the proper instructions on how to secure the wood and handle the tool in the most efficient way. They may not have been shown how to use appropriate guides and clamping techniques or were taught what qualities must be sought in the wood to ease the work. If they had received proper instruction in these things, they would have discovered that hand saws actually do most of the work for you; that a hand plane takes very little effort to remove a full-length shaving along the edge of the board as it produces a perfectly straight and mirror-smooth finish; and that chisels can quickly and precisely shave an edge to a perfect fit, even across end grain.

What can I build with handtools? (Can you really build anything substantial in a reasonable amount of time and effort without resorting to power tools?)

When I was a kid growing up in Western Massachusetts (this was in the early 1950's), I watched a neighbor — an elderly but sprightly carpenter — build a house for he and his wife. I was fascinated by the project and often went across the street right after school to see what he had done

An alder step stool with the tools used to build it.

PHOTO COURTESY OF THE COLONIAL WILLIAMSBURG FOUNDATION

that day. I remember being amazed that this guy, working alone, could build such a large object by himself. It wasn't until I got into the trade myself in the late 60's, however, that I realized something else amazing about him: he was building the house entirely without power tools! The only tools I saw (or heard) him use were some handsaws, a hand brace and a hammer.

In a way, though, I shouldn't have been amazed — he was old enough to have been in the generation of joiners who learned their trade before the advent of powered hand tools. The fact is, tradesmen like him had built all the cities east of Mississippi River prior to the Civil War with hand tools. And not just the houses, but also all the docks and the boats tied to them, all the commercial buildings, and all the furnishings inside them! Some of these furnishings — such as the Highboys of certain Philadelphian furniture makers — are now considered to be the pinnacle of American craftsmanship and design.

How much space will I need? (Aren't home wood-working shops pretty big, often taking up two-car garages or full basements?)

When I was doing research for *The Toolbox Book* several years ago, I had the good fortune of spending some time at Williamsburg — the restored early American village and working museum in Virginia. Under construction in the cabinetshop was, among other projects, one of the

A preindustrial, production cabinetmaker's shop — reconstructed at Colonial Williamsburg Village in Virginia.

aforementioned Highboys. While I found it fascinating to watch the work being done with hand tools, I was also amazed by the fact that there were at least a half-dozen artisans at work in the surprisingly tidy shop — all quietly conversing with each other and with the visitors. But it wasn't just the quiet or lack of dust that got me. It was also the fact that all this was going on in less floor space than a typical modern living room!

So it's really not out of the question that you could set up a hand tool-primary woodworking shop in a room in your house. What makes this possible is the absence of machinery — especially the space-hungry table saw, jointer, and surface planer — and the dust collection system necessary to cope with their by-products. As you will see in the first section of this book, all you need to make room for in your hand tool-primary shop is:

• A workbench for joinery and planing work.
• A low horse for hand sawing stock to rough dimensions.
• A bit of wall space to stack project lumber against.
• A few shelves of storage space above the bench for the hand tools.

But enough talk … let's get your shop up and running!

SECTION ONE

THE SHOP

The hand tool-primary woodworking shop is a pleasant place to hang out.
Because hand tools don't produce dust (they make only shavings), there
aren't slippery layers of dust overlying everything. Instead of the angry
screams of machines milling wood in front of your face, pleasant music
or conversation can provide the sound track of your time in the shop.
The absence of machine stations also means you won't be hoofing wood
around the shop all day — instead, you can settle in at a workbench with
the material and tools you'll be working with just a hand reach away.

Here at the Port Townsend School of Woodworking, up to eight people can work without crowding, never wearing dust
masks or earplugs as they converse pleasantly amongst themselves as each builds a project at his or her bench.

Size and Infrastructure Requirements

When you work wood primarily with hand tools you don't need a lot of space or infrastructure. Just as in the days of Colonial America, your workshop could simply be a spare room in your house as it was for the Dominy family of Long Island. You won't need much space — because it's the machines that take up so much room in the typical power tool shop. It's not just the machine's footprint, they also need a lot of space around them. In working with stationary machines you constantly have to move the wood past the machines rather than move the tools along the wood at a singular workstation (your workbench.) You also won't need sound insulation or dust control, because it's the machines that produce high levels of noise and clouds of dust. You won't need electric service beyond providing lighting … because it's the machines … well, you know the rest of the story.

If you do choose to have stationary machines for initial dimensioning of stock (such as a jointer-planer and a band saw) you can locate them in a garage or basement to maximize the floor space and to minimize noise and dust in your bench room. You can get away with this differentiation of space because, in hand tool-primary woodworking, we do not need constant, ready access to these tools as we do in machine-primary woodworking. You don't even need to control the temperature in the machine room (beyond preventing dew from forming on the metal surfaces). You won't be keeping the wood here or having to spend much time here yourself — you're only processing the wood on the way into the bench room.

The Size of Your Bench Room

If you are already familiar with machine-tool woodworking, you will likely be surprised to learn that you can create a completely adequate hand tool shop in a room the size of a typical master bedroom — perhaps as small as 150 square feet if you can avoid storing your excess lumber there. I have worked for more than a decade in a basement shop measuring 18 ft. × 28 ft. — and I've built all manner of furniture pieces and even an 18 ft. row boat in that space! With that much room, I do have a band saw for resawing lumber (to create book-matched panels) and for occasionally ripping long stock to width. My excuse is that I do build boats occasionally, which requires ripping long planks to gentle curves with changing bevels. When making furniture,

The Dominy shop. Restoration of 18th century clock and cabinetmakers shop by Winterthur Museum.

you rarely need to rip a board longer than 4', and that just takes about a minute with a sharp rip saw. Because I generally buy my lumber pre-dimensioned to thickness from a local hardwood supplier, I no longer need a surface planer. I also do without a table saw or panel saw as I no longer work with plywood, and I do all my joinery with hand tools. The absence of a jointer, a surface planer and a table saw frees up an enormous amount of room in my modest-sized basement shop.

My woodshop is now a spacious, warm and pleasant place to work. I'm often joined there by the family dog (who loves to gnaw on off-cuts) and youngsters (who get to work at the low assembly table at which I've installed a vise for just that purpose). Now that only hand tools operate here (with a

I spend many pleasant evenings working in my basement shop, often with my two helpers.

very occasional run on the band saw, drill press or lathe), there is little dust, noise or danger that would make it unsafe for them. I also get to listen to the radio and actually hear the lyrics of the songs!

In the summer, I create a second bench room on our home's 8' × 12' front porch! If you have a porch, I highly recommend you try it. I simply set up a workbench and, drawing from a carry-tote full of planes and saws, I smooth boards and cut and fit joints to my heart's content into the long summer twilight. The neighbors don't object (there's no noise or clouds of dust flying about) and in fact, they like to watch. I do usually move back inside for final assembly work where I have more room.

Heat and Plumbing

One of the biggest advantages of being able to work inside the home (or in an easily heated small workspace) is the fact that you can usually easily acclimatize the space to the same temperature and humidity levels as the rest of the house. That not only creates a pleasant environment for you to work in, but it creates a perfect environment for the furniture pieces you build. Here you not only acclimate the wood prior to

Wood near heater — an example of where not to store wood.

the building process (see Acclimating the Wood on page 77), but you continue to work with the wood in the same conditions in which it will live out its life as a piece of furniture. Because this minimizes dimensional changes that otherwise often occur when wood is moved from the typical cooler and damper machine-room workshops to a warm and dry home, it goes a long way toward ensuring joints will stay closed, surfaces will stay flat and split-free and the piece will endure.

If you have a source of direct heat in the shop (such as a hot air vent or a heat stove) as opposed to uniform heat (such as in-floor heating pipes), be careful not to place your lumber anywhere near the heat source or it will likely become too dry. Whatever the heat source, avoid storing lumber near the ceiling as that area is hotter and drier than the environment in which the furniture piece will live. If you store your lumber on end (and I sometimes do), it's a good idea to get into the habit of turning it end-for-end occasionally to avoid having one end (the ceiling end) drying out more than the other.

The only reason you might need plumbing in or close to your bench room is to provide water for your sharpening station (assuming you are using waterstones). While it is easier to rinse stones and jigs off at a sink, you can get by with a plant mister (get a big one with a largish squeeze handle) and a bucket in which to swish the stones and the tools during the sharpening process.

Lighting — Natural and Man-made

While "the more light the better" is generally a good thing, in hand tool woodworking the direction of the light tends to be more important than the intensity of the ambient light. Traditionally (before electricity), windows provided nearly all the light for the artisans at their workbenches. If I were to depend on only natural light, I would have large, south-facing windows to invite in the direct rays of the sun. The high intensity, high contrast light would fall across the benches (which I would set perpendicular to the rays) so I could clearly see the scribed layout lines, tear-out, and the ridges and hollows on the surfaces as I planed the wood flat and smooth. Light from the upper portion of North-facing windows would reflect off my whitewashed ceiling, providing ample ambient light.

In both my shop (above) and the historically recreated Hays cabinetshop at Williamsburg, notice that the tools are kept out where they can be easily seen and reached. Also notice the lack of dust — not because they just cleaned up, but because the woodworkers are using cutting tools, not abrading tools!

If you don't have windows, or if they are too small or poorly oriented to let in much natural light (and, of course, if you want to work at night!), you can install swing-arm lamps on the bench and/or set up photo-type lamps on tripods. I often use a combination of both as evening sets in. Orient the lights as necessary to cast light at low angles across the work pieces so that cut lines or grooves in the wood cast easy-to-see shadows.

To provide ambient light, I usually install a mix of incandescent and tube fluorescent lamps in the ceiling to provide warm, relatively shadow-free lighting throughout the shop. You may need to add additional ceiling lamps in the area over the assembly table so you clearly view a project under construction. Avoid placing just one light directly over the table — instead, try to illuminate it from a variety of angles so that you can see in and around the piece as you assemble it. At times, you may find the need to bring over a lamp on a tripod to get light deeper inside an assembly.

Shop Layout

Historically, artisans kept their tools in chests, hung them on wall pegs and set them on open shelves below or near the workbench. Tools needed for the task at hand would be out on the bench throughout the day but were always returned to the chest, shelves or pegs at the end of the workday (usually when the sun went down) in order to clear the bench of shavings. This prevented tools from being lost in the shavings and it made them easy to find and reach when needed for the next day's work. Just a glance told the artisan if the tool he wanted was already out on the bench — and if it weren't, he would know exactly where to find it (which in the hand tool shop is usually only a step away from the bench).

In my "New Traditional" shop I also keep most of my everyday tools on open shelves, racks and pegs set

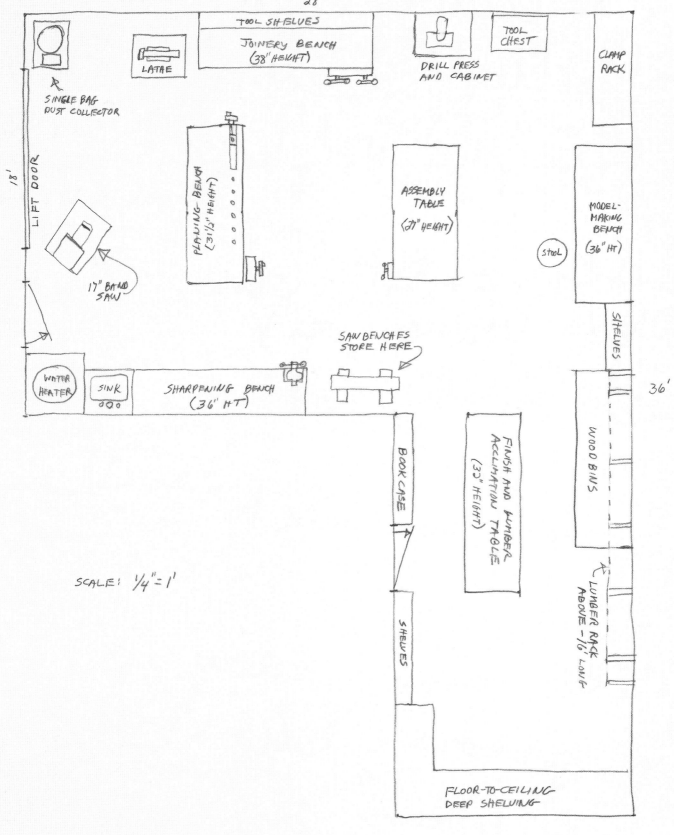

28'

TOOL SHELVES

JOINERY BENCH
(38" HEIGHT)

TOOL CHEST

DRILL PRESS AND CABINET

CLAMP RACK

LATHE

SINGLE BAG DUST COLLECTOR

18'

LIFT DOOR

PLANING BENCH
(31½" HEIGHT)

ASSEMBLY TABLE
(27" HEIGHT)

STOOL

MODEL-MAKING BENCH
(36" HT)

17" BAND SAW

SHELVES

SAW BENCHES STORE HERE

36'

WATER HEATER

SINK

SHARPENING BENCH
(36" HT)

WOOD BINS

FINISH AND LUMBER ACCLIMATION TABLE
(35" HEIGHT)

BOOK CASE

LUMBER RACK ABOVE - 16' LONG

SCALE: ¼" = 1'

SHELVES

FLOOR-TO-CEILING DEEP SHELVING

LAYOUT OF MY SHOP IN MY "NEW TRADITIONAL" STYLE

within a step or so of my two primary workbenches. When my shop was machine-tool oriented, I kept almost all my tools in drawers or in wall hung cabinets behind doors to keep out the dust. Now that I'm making hardly any dust, coupled with the fact that my hand tools are actually getting into my hands on a daily basis, I find it much more efficient to keep most of them out in the open.

Referring to drawing on the previous page to keep oriented, let's take a walk through my shop to see how I've laid out my workbenches, the three stationary power tools, and the various storage areas and open spaces.

Except for the drill press, I've clustered my other stationary tools (below) into the southeast corner of my shop and set as closely as possible to the walls. This maximizes my floor space and minimizes the length of run between the band saw and the lathe to the upright dust collector tucked into the corner. If I need to run boards longer than about 6' (which almost never happens when building furniture) I've carefully situated the band saw (which is bolted to the floor for stability) so I can open the overhead garage door and run the stock through to the outside. I've seen some shops, lacking a door or window in the right place, feature a just-big-enough pass-through cut into the wall for that purpose.

Moving to the south wall of the shop, you can see (bottom) where I keep nearly all my everyday hand tools: right over my dedicated joinery bench on open shelves or below in open cabinets. I place most of my

Southeast corner of shop — a cluster of stationary tools and dust collector.

South wall of shop — joinery bench, drill press.

layout tools, chisels, rasps, trimming and joinery planes and backsaws above the bench where I can easily reach them. I keep most of my planes for dimensioning, truing and smoothing on the open shelves below the bench where they are just a step away from my Roubo-style planing bench. I keep panel saws for coarse cutting here as they are just a step away from where I set up my sawbenches when cutting stock to length and width. Finally, in the larger open area below the double-screw vise, I keep the joinery bench's essential shop-made fixtures: bench hooks, miter boxes and shooting boards.

To the right of the bench you'll find my drill press and the cabinets that hold its drill bits and other accessories, including a drawer full of braces and bits for hand drilling. A shop vacuum sits to the side of the press to pick up most of its dust, as well as being handy to pick up shavings produced on the joinery bench. The location of the press here wasn't arbitrary. As part of the tooling in the joinery process (making holes for mortises), its just a step away from the joinery

Western portion of shop — assembly table; clamp rack; metalworking and model-making bench.

bench where I trim up the mortise and tenons. It's also just a step away from my metalworking area where the drill press often serves to make fastening holes in hardware or shop-made tools and fixtures.

The western portion of my shop (shown above) is where projects come together. Here I've installed a dedicated, low assembly table at just the right height for assembling most of my furniture pieces. I've learned long ago that standard-sized workbenches are too high and usually too narrow to accommodate the assembly process for most furniture projects. The bench is also the perfect height for kids to work at, and I've installed a vise on the table for just that purpose. You can, of course, get away without a dedicated assembly bench by using low sawhorses to support the work — though you'll find the flat surface of the bench, if trued flat, a real boon to assembly work.

I've left ample space around the bench so I can get at all sides of the project as necessary. I keep tools associated with the assembly process (such as mallets, glue and glue applicators, screwdrivers, wrenches and socket sets, hardware layout jigs, etc.) in the table's deep, full-extension drawers. A step away in the southwest corner of the shop is my floor-to-ceiling clamp rack, bristling with a wide array of clamping tools.

Just beyond the assembly table and set against the west wall of the shop is my general-purpose workbench. Here

I do metalwork, occasionally carve in three dimensions, and build and repair boat and airplane models. Open shelves above hold metalworking and modelmaking tools; a variety of electric drills, drivers and chargers; and miscellaneous fasteners.

Looking toward the northeast side of the shop (top left), my low and massive planing bench plants itself firmly in the middle of the room. East-facing windows cast natural light over the bench during the day while a bar of task lights and a swing arm lamp provide additional light so I can clearly see the planing tracks made during smoothing operations. My rather extensive sharpening station — a long bench set above storage cabinets — sits against the north wall of the shop, running into the utility sink in the corner. The cabinets contain a large variety of accessories for the sharpening equipment, some finishing supplies and larger hardware items.

In the northwest corner of the workspace (bottom left), I'm fortunate to have an L-shaped extension in which I can store lumber and other materials as well as providing an open space for a variety of purposes as I describe below. Wall-mounted lumber racks hold some prized boards that I've hoarded over the years while shop-made wood bins sit below in a purpose-made bin to organize short offcuts — mostly by size.

At the moment I'm using the open space in the L to accommodate an 8'-long bench on which I'm acclimating some lumber for my next project — a very important part of the furniture-making process. I also use this bench to support a line of bar clamps for gluing up long edge-laminated assemblies such as tabletops. When I need open space, I'll knock down the bench to create an assembly area for larger projects; to store larger furniture projects and components during the construction process; or as an area away from the bench room to apply wipe-on oil or shellac finishes.

North-eastern portion of shop — planing bench and sharpening station with sink.

Looking into the "L" — lumber storage and acclimation bench.

Workbenches

In traditional Western-style woodworking, the workbench was central to nearly all the woodworking processes. This is where the artisan planed surfaces and trued edges; ripped and crosscut short lengths of stock to size (with smaller-sized panel saws or bow saws); made precision cuts for joints (with backsaws); pared joints; chopped out mortises and put together smaller assemblies such as drawers. As a new traditional woodworker, this is where you will be spending more than 90 percent of your time as well.

As you might rightly assume, it's crucial to choose the right type and size of bench to accommodate you and the kind of work you intend to do at the bench. There are many styles of benches to choose from (see the drawing below). Some, like the low-slung and massive Roubo and English-syle benches. lean more toward accommodating planing and coarser joinery work (such as chopping out mortises) while the typical northern European "Continental" benches with their higher stature and large shoulder vises lean more toward accommodating cabinetmaker's performing finer joinery (such as sawing out dovetails and other close, precise work). Of course, any type of bench can be set up with fixtures (such as vises, various planing stops and sawing guides) to allow most any kind of process.

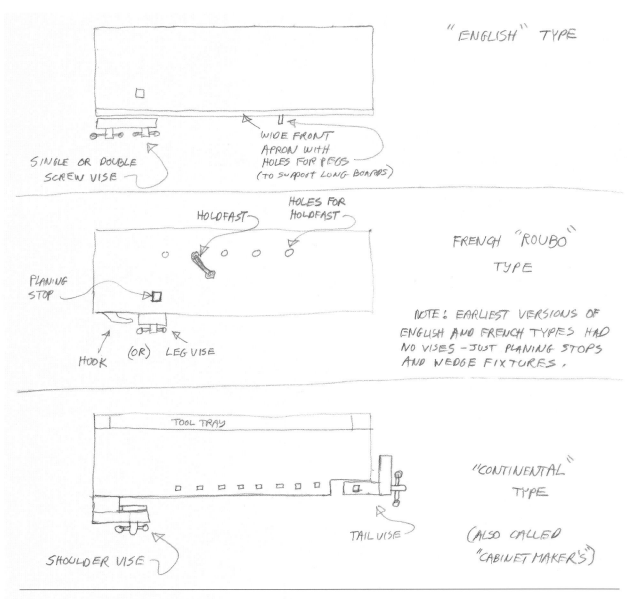

TYPES OF TRADITIONAL WORKBENCHES

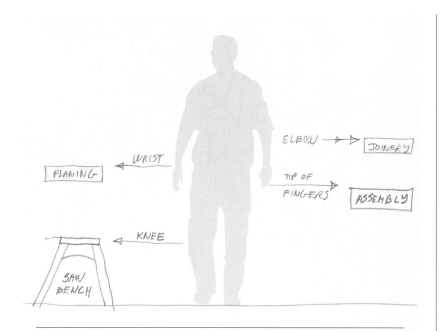

THE ILLUSTRATION SHOWS THE BEST HEIGHTS FOR BENCHES, IN RELATION TO BODY ANATOMY, DURING VARIOUS OPERATIONS

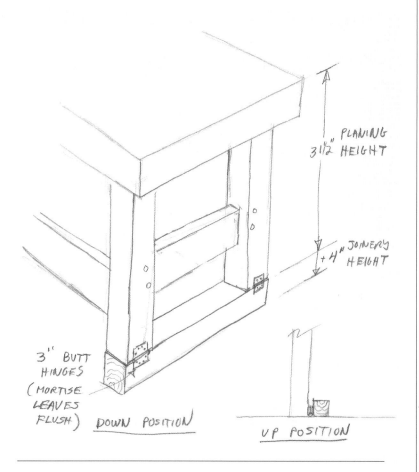

SWING-DOWN BENCH LEG SUPPORTS

I think the most crucial thing to determine about a bench is to find the right work surface height. It's got to be low enough so you can plane boards comfortably with your upper body weight bearing above the plane (and low enough so you can chop out mortises with your shoulders well above the mallet), yet the bench must not be so low that you'll find it uncomfortable to stand and make precision saw and paring cuts. In these latter operations the bench must support the wood high enough so you can see the cut lines and so you can operate the backsaws, paring chisels and trimming planes without stooping. Unfortunately, because of the shape of the human body, it's literally impossible for a bench to meet all these requirements.

There are however, some ways around it. When you are young, strong and flexible, it's not such a problem to work at a bench whose height falls somewhere in the middle of the two ideals. For most people, this height comes to wrist height (see the drawing at top left). For myself, I find that I simply can't work with this compromise. A height that allows me to put my fairly light frame to bear over a handplane (and my aging muscles need all the help from my body mass) is far too low to hold work where my aging eyes can see the cut lines for precision work. And my back is long past the point of holding up for more than a minute or so of stooping.

As you've already discovered (in the discussion above about my shop layout) my solution for this problem was to build two benches — one dedicated to planing and coarse joinery work (such as chopping out mortises) and the other for precision work (such as cutting dovetails). As you can see in the drawing at top left, the planing bench comes up to wrist height while the joinery bench is at or just below elbow height. The saw bench for coarse ripping and crosscutting comes to knee height (more on this bench later). I set the benches a step away from each other and therefore just a step away from the tools used at either of them. You should, of course, take these height suggestions as a starting point since everyone's body frame and musculature is unique.

If you don't have the time, space or inclination to build separate benches for planing and joinery, there is another solution available (other than being young, that is). It's a simple matter to rig a pair of swing down leg stanchions that will allow you to quickly change the height of the bench as necessary. (See the drawing at left, bottom). To use the stanchions to raise the bench, you lift one end of the bench at a time, allowing gravity (and perhaps a little help from your foot) to let the stanchions swing down under the fixed leg support base or posts. Reverse the procedure to lower the bench.

The bottom line, however, is that no matter which type of bench you choose, it should meet three fundamental criteria. First: The top should be dead flat (if it isn't, and it's wood, you can flatten it with hand planes following the same process shown on page 169). Second: The bench should be sturdy enough to not shake when you plane or saw a board on it. Vibration absorbs energy and slows the process. Third: It should be the right height for the work at hand. You don't

need to start with an expensive bench with massive vises — the various bench accessories that I show you how to make in the next section of the book allow you to work effectively at the most basic bench with a simple bolt-on vise.

Dedicated Planing Bench

Because I could dedicate one of my benches for mostly hand planing (I also chop mortises and crosscut smaller stock to length here) I decided to go with a narrow, free-standing, French-style "Roubo" bench I made by fitting a massive, timber-frame like base to a commercially made, 4"-thick hard maple top. (See the source in the Resources). Three things about this type of bench make it the appropriate choice for hand planing: It's massive (as in: this bench-will-never-move massive); it stands much lower than most typical commercial benches (in my case, 31½" from the

With a frame featuring massive timbers joined with pegged mortise and tenon joints and a top made from 4" thick hard maple, my planing bench will be as solid as a tree stump under the most vigorous planing action. The top, as well as the shoulder and tail vise hardware, were manufactured by Jameel Abraham of "Benchcrafted" — see the Resources for contact information.

floor to the top of the bench); and it's narrow and free-standing so I can plane boards from a variety of directions without having to re-orient the board.

All of these attributes are crucial to the comfortable and productive planing of boards: First, the rigidity and mass of the bench allows you to

The planing bench also offers a rock solid support for heavy chisel work — in this case, chopping out a mortise.

transfer all the energy from the plane into the wood (and not into energy-absorbing racking motions). Second, the low height allows you to keep your upper body mass bearing down on the plane to keep it in the cut (lowering the amount of energy you would otherwise expend if just your muscles were in play). Even when planing long boards, it's a piece of cake: You simply walk along holding the plane with your shoulder oriented over the tool — the inertia of your upper body coupled with your forward momentum does almost all the work. (See the picture on page 23). Finally, the fact that the bench allows you to plane boards held in the tail vise from either side means you don't have to constantly shift the board around when making diagonal passes during the flattening procedure. (You'll find a full description of this process in the second section of this book).

The mass and height of this bench also make it the perfect fixture for holding stock while chopping out mortises with a mortise chisel. The low height again allows me to position most of my upper body above the workpiece so I can use body mass and not just musculature to deliver the mallet blows while the stump-like mass of this bench ensures that all the energy and motion from the chisel goes into the wood, not into flexing the bench. In the picture at left, notice that I've located the workpiece so that the mortise hole-to-be falls directly over one of the massive bench legs. This is probably a bit of overkill as the 4"-thick hard maple top doesn't flex all that much in itself — in fact, it doesn't flex at all!

Dedicated Joinery Bench

Because I could dedicate this bench (top right) to joinery, I was able to set it much higher than the Roubo planing bench: 38" from floor to benchtop. That's so high it's actually difficult for me to get used to looking at it — you never see commercial benches that high! Also, because I don't have to work at this bench from any side other than its front, I was able to mount it to the wall — a strategy that allowed me to build the bench lighter (cheaper and easier) without sacrificing rigidity.

Equipped with a twin-screw vise at the front right side and augmented with a variety of bench hooks and saw fixtures, I find this bench to be absolutely perfect for what I primarily use it for: precision crosscutting of parts; sawing and paring

My second bench, set much higher than the planing bench and featuring a double-screw vise, is set up primarily for sawing and paring joints.

joints in end grain (dovetail joints and tenons); and holding smaller stock upright for ripping with a small panel saw. As you can see in the photo at right I secure the stock to the right-hand side of the vise so that the waste falls to the right of the cutline — this puts the cut line between the saw blade and my line of sight. If I were left handed, by the way, I would have placed the twin-screw vise on the left-hand side.

Bench Accessories

The fixtures shown in the photos on page 26 are mostly shop-made accessories that would be found at most joiner's benches. They add significantly to the speed and accuracy of using bench saws and bench planes. Many are simply and quickly secured to the bench with one of the bench's vises and/or a holdfast fitted into one of the bench holes. As you follow through the rest of the book, you will learn how to make and use some of these fixtures as well as some essential layout tools. At the same time, you will learn how

Because the twin-screw vise comes flush with the side of the bench, it can grasp a board vertically for ripping.

to use nearly all the hand tools of the traditional woodworking artisan as you produce flat surfaces, true edges, smooth curves and produce essential joints such as dadoes and rabbets.

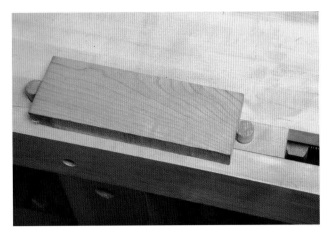

Bench dogs fit into holes drilled (sometimes square holes chiseled) into the bench top and the tail vise along the centerline of the tail vise's clamping direction. There are commonly used to capture and secure a board flat on the face of the bench.

A **holdfast**, made from wrought or spring steel, wedges into a hole in the benchtop to secure a board or a bench accessory to the bench. One whack of a mallet to the top of the holdfast locks it down — a tap on the back releases it.

By slipping a board on its edge into the V-shaped cutout of an **edge-planing stop** (which is, in turn, secured in a vise), you can almost instantly secure a narrow board for planing. A wedge prevents the board from shifting. In this photo, a longer board is additionally secured from shifting sideways by the addition of a board trapped under a holdfast.

A **face-planing stop** secures into the side vise of the bench provides a nearly instantaneous backstop for face planing a board.

A **sticking board** supports long narrow boards so that their long edges are held up off the bench, allowing you to use a plane to make rabbets, grooves or profiles along the edge. A screw head prevents the board from sliding forward.

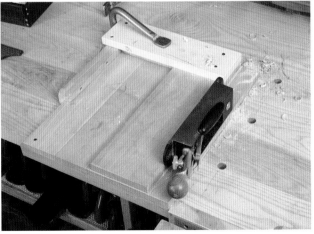

This fixture — a **shooting board** — allows you to quickly plane a true edge on the end of a board. The plane shown in the photo is a dedicated shooting plane, though any bench plane with a square shoulder will do the job

Sawbench Pair

For the years I worked with sawhorses on job sites doing finish carpentry, I never thought twice about them — until I went to use a pair for ripping a board by hand. For this purpose they were essentially useless. The problem with typical sawhorses (industrial-era sawhorses that is), is their height. They are designed to hold workpieces at a convenient height for pushing power tools such as routers and circular saws across the wood. But when you want to move your arm back and forth to power a handsaw, the height is far too high for the way our bodies work forcing us to take only very short strokes. No wonder everyone who has tried to saw a board by hand on standard sawhorses has come away saying "handsaws are too dang slow!" (Of course, most handsaws on today's typical job sites are rarely in good condition — but that's another story.)

The sawhorse pair shown here (which artisans used to call sawbenches) are much lower. They are sized to my body (the height of my kneecap), which makes them the perfect height for supporting a board clamped underneath my knee, and allows my arm to push a saw to the full length of its blade without imparting any twist. (Saw manufacturers traditionally made handsaws to the length of an average man's arm, which also happens to be his full forward-and-back arm movement — an average of 26"). With a freshly sharpened 8-point crosscut saw, I can crosscut a ¾"-thick pine board within seconds of the speed of a power saw — about 4" per second. Thicker and harder wood does take a bit longer but, (and you may find this hard to believe if you've never used a truly sharp handsaw in combination with a true pair of sawbenches) it's far more enjoyable and not all that much slower! A measured drawing of my sawbench pair appears on page 165.

Built low enough to help you gain the most powerful and efficient stroke possible with a traditional panel saw, these sawbenches support the stock for cutting stock to approximate length and width. Note that I've made the inside legs of the benches facing one another almost perpendicular to the floor — this feature gets them out of the way of the rip saw which runs lengthwise between the two horses.

I set the perpendicular legs facing toward the waste side of a crosscut to get them out of the way of the saw, yet supporting the wood right next to the cut, reducing energy-wasting vibration.

My shop-made assembly table sits nearly at the center of my shop with access from all sides. Its height (about 27") and its area (3' x 6') are just right for me to do glue-ups and to assembly most pieces of furniture without stooping or having to climb up on a stool.

Assembly Table

If you've ever struggled to build a project on top of a standard bench — or worse, on a piece of plywood laid on the floor — you will really appreciate a table that's sized specifically for you to comfortably and efficiently assemble most typical furniture pieces. The table I built for my shop is at exactly the right height (it comes to the bottom of my fingers when I stand upright) and the right dimensions (3' × 6') for me to assemble most of the projects I build with a minimum of stooping or over-reaching. Built heavy and sturdy with drawbored mortise-and-tenon joints, this table never shakes under any assembly procedure. Equipped with large, deep drawers and an open space behind a frame-and-panel door, most of the tools I need for assembly work are right where I need them. If space in your shop is at a premium, you can create an adequate assembly area by laying boards across your pair of sawbenches.

Hand-powered Tools

To give you a fundamental understanding of hand tools — I present the tools of the trade grouped into their common general function and then explain three things about them: What the tool does, how it does it, and which ones are essential for working wood to build furniture primarily by hand. But learning to use hand tools the right way isn't enough — you need to know why it's the right way. I have found that people more quickly grasp how to choose and use a tool when they learn not just a rote prescription, but rather a basic understanding of the physics underlying how a tool works. Specifics on how to use the tool will be covered in detail in the project section of the book as the work to be done calls for the tool.

Before we start, though, you should know that when purchasing hand tools you really do get what you pay for. When you pay home and gar-

den store prices, what you get are tools that are — how can I put this delicately — garden variety. These are tools that might work for making garden stakes, but they don't work well for making furniture. When buying from specialized tool dealers and manufacturers (see the source list on page 175), you will absolutely pay more money, but you get tools that, when sharpened and tuned properly, cut and saw wood much better and go longer between sharpenings. The problem with cheap tools (and cheap copies of expensive tools) is primarily one of sloppy tolerances and poor engineering. The garden-store, garden-variety hand tools generally don't offer steel that stays sharp or, in the case of handplanes, a platform that holds the blades securely and precisely oriented. Lacking these features, inexpensive tools can never perform as well as the "real" thing. The real thing, by the way, includes not just new, premium-grade tools, but also properly restored, mostly pre-World War II equipment.

WHY ONLY WESTERN-STYLE TOOLS?

I'm sure it has become readily apparent to you by this point that there has been no discussion of Japanese tools. Its not that I don't like using Japanese tools (I have used their saws, hammers and chisels for many years), it's that I don't want to discuss them unless I'm going to teach Eastern-style woodworking comprehensively — which I am absolutely not qualified to do. The problem is that Western and Eastern artisans took an opposite approach to dealing with sawing and planing wood: The former push their saws and planes while the latter pull them.

At first thought, pushing versus pulling might seem like just a simple difference in work style — but in reality the difference is profound. Designing tools to be pulled through the wood affects how their handles and blades are shaped; how the tools are held relative to the workpiece; and how the artisan holds his or her body when using them. When added up, that's an awful lot of difference!

Traditional Asian woodworkers held their work and positioned their bodies mostly around floor-based positions to maximize the efficiency of their tools. Working on the floor at an angled beam for a bench, they could use gravity and the large muscles of the back to help while sawing and planing while their legs and feet were freed up to be used as clamps to hold the wood. Western joiners and cabinetmakers traditionally worked upright at level benches augmented with vises and other mechanical holddowns. (There is an exception: chairmakers and wainwrights often sat at a shaving horse and pulled drawknives and spokeshaves while using their feet on a lever clamp — but that's another book!). There are also significant differences in the way the plane and chisel irons are honed and the way saws are sharpened between the two realms. To keep the learning curve as flat and smooth as possible, I've decided to keep my teaching oriented to the Western style of working wood by hand.

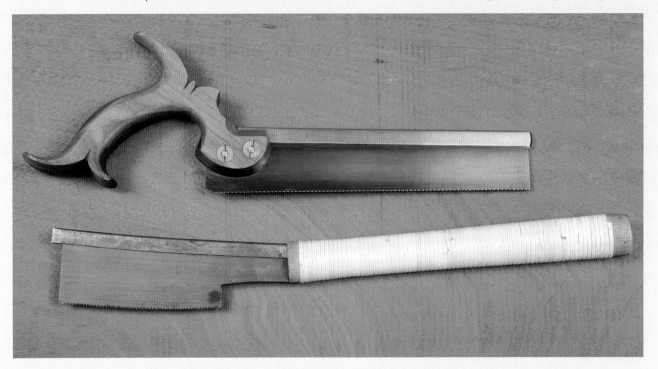

Tools for Defining Where to Remove Wood — Layout Tools

Layout implements are the first tools you'll use in the woodworking process. With them, you'll lay out and mark highly-precise reference lines to show you where, exactly, to cut the wood to bring it to a certain size or shape.

Marking Gauges

WHAT THEY DO:

A marking gauge transfers a known reference surface (such as the trued edge or end of a board) to a parallel, visible guide line. Most commonly, you'll use this line to indicate where to rip a board to width; to set the shoulder line of joints (such as a tenon or a dovetail); to mark the sides of mortise; and to mark the extent of a rabbet's width and depth.

HOW THEY DO IT:

A sliding head with a trued, flat face rides on a beam that contains either a sharp pin (sometimes two pins in the case of a mortise-marking gauge), a cutter or a pencil. To make a mark a certain distance from a reference surface, you slide the head along the beam and then lock it down when the face of the head is at the required distance from the marking pin or cutter. In traditional hand tool woodworking, this setting is almost never made to a numbered dimension — instead, it's set by holding it to a workpiece to be fitted or, for a mortise, to the sides of a chisel.

WHICH ONES YOU NEED:

You can, for a while, get away with just one: a gauge with a single cutter blade. The cutter will cut beautifully across the grain, but it won't work quite as well with the grain as the pin-type gauges. (You simply take a couple of shallow cuts to compensate). Upgrade to a double-pin mortise gauge to speed up the layout of mortises, and consider a panel gauge for quickly laying out rip cuts on wider boards.

Cluster of marking gauges: single pin; double pin; single cutter; panel gauge.

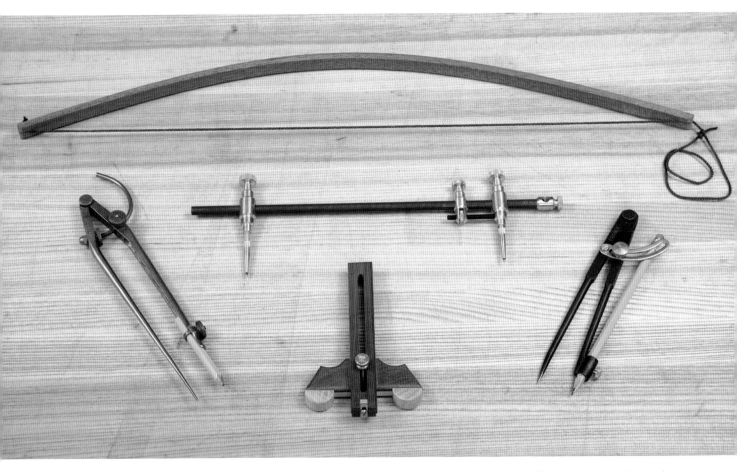

Layout Tools for Curved Lines

WHAT THEY DO:

The compass and the trammel points create a circle of any size referenced to a certain focal point. A bow enables you to draw a portion of a circle (or a curve of changing radius) anywhere on the face of a board without the need for a fixed focus point. A marking gauge with a customized head (the face has two reference points instead of a flat plane) transfers a curved edge.

HOW THEY DO IT:

The compass and trammels have two points: one is set at the focal point of the circle while the other is free to swing and mark the circumference of the circle at a fixed radius. The bows are bent and held by a string to produce an arc along their length. If the bow is asymmetric in thickness, the arc it produces will constantly change in radius, producing a pleasing "French" curve. I customized the face of the marking gauge so it indexes the marking point to two points rather than a flat surface, allowing the face to index to a curved edge.

Compass (large and small), trammel points, shop-made curved bow, customized marking gauge for marking along a curved edge.

WHICH ONES YOU NEED:

A compass with a 6" sweep is all you need for most traditional furniture making where you are just laying out rounded corners. If, however, you want to make a large circle, say to lay out a round table, then trammel points (which can be affixed to any length stick) are essential. If you need a rabbet to run parallel to a curve, it's a simple matter to customize the face of a marking gauge by adding two half-dowels to either side of the beam. If, at some point, you move away from rectilinear furniture, you will want to have a set of bows — they are available commercially in fiberglass, or you can make up your own with lengths of straight-grained wood and a string.

Squares and Bevel Gauges

WHAT THEY DO:

The head and the tongue of a square are accurately set at a fixed angle to one another (perpendicular or at 45°) and therefore act as templates for laying out that angle on the work. Some feature sliding tongues that allow you to use the tool as a marking gauge — or to adjust the tongue to act as a feeler or marking gauge in conjunction with a pencil. The bevel gauge features a tongue that is adjustable in angle to the head.

HOW THEY DO IT:

The head of a try square or bevel gauge (as opposed to carpenter's framing squares) is made thicker than the blade so you can set the tool on the face of a board with the head referenced to the board's edge while the tongue lies flat on the face. This allows you to mark accurately along the tongue to transfer the tools inherent angle.

Small engineers T-square; wide base square; combination 12" and 18", traditional, shop-made try square, adjustable bevel gauge.

WHICH ONES YOU NEED:

You can get away with just two: a 12" combination square and a 6" bevel gauge. Later, to make it easier to lay out small joints, you may want to add (or make) a smaller version — and a larger version for laying out crosscuts on wide boards. A wide-base machinist's square is a luxury for indexing long bits during the drilling process.

Marking knives, awls (large and small), mechanical pencil, fine point gel pen, grease "China" pencil.

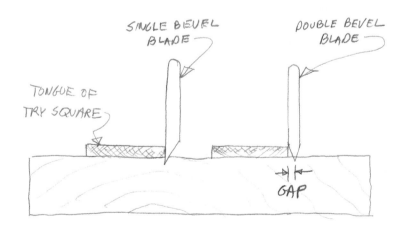

SINGLE BEVEL VS. DOUBLE BEVEL

Marking Tools

WHAT THEY DO:

A marking knife (also called a "striking" knife) establishes a reference line that can also act as a miniature tool track. (As you will see later, tool tracks are essential to precision sawing and paring.) An awl makes a pinprick in the wood to locate, for example, the lead point of a drill bit. Pens and pencils make the cutlines visible to aging eyes and/or when working in dim light. Grease pencils and lumber crayons create temporary, easily removed marks for labeling parts and indicating reference versus non-reference surfaces.

HOW THEY DO IT:

You know how pens, pencils and crayons work, but a marking knife could use a little explanation. For use as a precision layout tool, a knife should have a single beveled edge (most knife edges have two bevels). This allows you to hold the flat side of the knife upright against a reference surface (usually the tongue of a square or bevel gauge) to ensure a precise transfer of that reference surface to the wood (see the drawing below left). Double bevel blades, unless carefully angled, may have a gap between the knife edge and the ruler.

WHICH ONES YOU NEED:

You can actually get away with a typical, garden-variety utility knife for layout work if you are aware of its double-bevel edge when holding it against your layout tool. When it gets dull you can quickly change the blade, and most feature an adjustable-length blade so you can reach deep into a recess if necessary (which occurs regularly when laying out narrow dovetails). But they aren't pretty and there is that accuracy problem — you'll want to add some wood-handled, woodworker's striking knives eventually (see the suppliers resource on page 175). Go to your local office supply outlet to get a good quality mechanical pencil and a stash of .5mm HB lead; a gel-type, fine point pen; and a handful of grease (sometimes called "China") pencils.

Dividers and Rulers

WHAT THEY DO:

You use dividers to fix (and to subsequently transfer in most cases) a certain distance between two points with absolute precision. During the construction process, dividers offer the most accurate and error-free way to transfer dimensions of components and to establish locations of joints. It is also a design tool. The most complex piece of furniture can be (and has been) designed and drawn out with dividers, sometimes coupled with a sector. For determining numerical measurements, I usually use a two-foot long folding rule.

The sector (I use the folding rule as a sector as well as a larger, shop-made version), offers a simple and foolproof way to divide a fixed dimension into whole-number segments or to scale a design up or down by changing the "base one" dimension.

HOW THEY DO IT:

A set of dividers, probably one of the most ancient layout tools, is simply a hinged pair of pins. The points, sharpened to stick into the wood to prevent slippage, spread apart to set out a certain distance while a swing arm with a bearing screw secure the points to that setting. If you want to repeat that distance along a line (straight or curved), you simply "walk" the dividers from pinprick to pinprick.

WHICH ONES YOU NEED:

Start with a pair of 6" dividers. Be sure to choose versions with a locking arm rather than just a high-friction-fit hinge point. If one of the legs has an attachment for holding a pencil, it can also serve as a compass. Later, as you find yourself moving away from measuring with numbers to using the traditional, fail-safe geometry of dividers for doing layouts and transferring dimensions and spacings, you will want a few smaller and a few larger ones. During a typical furniture project, you'll want to leave a few fixed to an oft-repeated setting (helpfully labeled with a piece of masking tape).

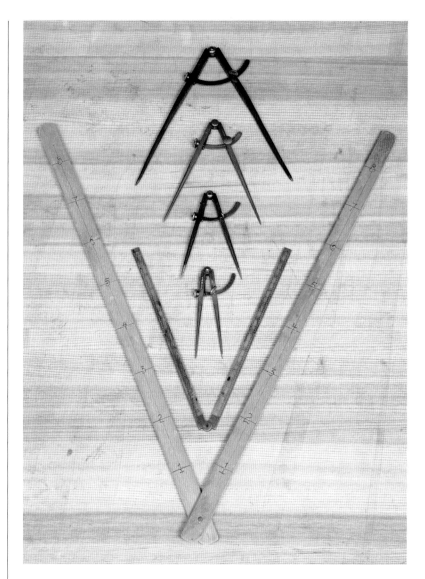

Dividers from large to small; two-foot folding rule; shop-made sector.

Tools for Changing the Size of the Board

The fastest way to change the size (and sometimes the shape) of a board is to whack off the parts that aren't the size (or shape) you want with a hatchet! In some woodworking trades (making wooden shoes, chairs from green wood or even in the making of small open boats) the hatchet was the primary tool — like a table saw is to a casework cabinetmaker today. The next fastest way to change a board in size is to separate it with a coarse-toothed saw. Finally, if there isn't that much to remove — say less than ½" from the width of a board — a highly aggressive plane can be called upon. While a hatchet can also do this task, it takes a good bit of experience and confidence to hack and hew close to a layout line. You could also saw off the narrow piece of waste right to the line, but ripsawing usually takes much longer than removing thick shavings with a scrub plane — plus the latter is far easier to resharpen than the former!

Carpenter's Axe

WHAT THEY DO:
In furniture work, you can use a joiner's hatchet (or carpenter's axe) to either hew away waste or to split a board in half (and half again and again as necessary to the required dimension is reached). These ancient tools work fast, but they require a deft hand and wood with straight grain to work with accuracy and to keep within the waste area. In the most experienced hands, you can split, then chop, and then shave the wood right to a cutline. (That wouldn't be me, by the way.)

HOW THEY DO IT:
The hatchet or axe features a wedge-shaped blade mounted to a handle for you to hold and power the cutting edge into the wood. To split the wood, the hatchet acts as a wedge as it enters the end grain of the board and separates the fibers longitudinally. In the hewing process, the hatchet acts more like a knife, slicing into the side of the fibers, allowing you to take off a controlled amount of material.

WHICH ONES YOU NEED:
Unless you intend to get into early traditional joinery work in which all the boards — from clapboards to tabletops — were split, rather than sawn to dimension, you can get away with just one. I use a Swedish-made carpenter's axe that features a shallow beveled and straight edged blade with a cutout that allows me to position my hand behind the blade for fine control. This type of axe works well for both hewing off material as well as splitting along the grain.

Handsaws

WHAT THEY DO:

Handsaws make a groove through the board (called a kerf) that separates a board into different widths, lengths or thickness. Because the teeth of full-sized panel saws are rather coarse (there are not many teeth per inch), they make fast, but rough-edged kerf cuts that need to be planed if they are to show or are to be fitted against another board.

HOW THEY DO IT:

The teeth of a handsaw either shear the fibers like knives when cutting across the grain or sever the fibers like a chisel when cutting (i.e. ripping) with the grain. The teeth have a set — they bend alternately a little to each side — to make the kerf slightly wider than the blade from which the teeth are made. In better saws, the blades are tapered in thickness. They are thinner away from the teeth, allowing less set. That improves the saw's performance because the less set, the narrower the kerf that is being made, and that requires less energy on your part to push the saw through the wood. Another performance-enhancing benefit is that the narrower kerf tends to act as a reference surface to guide the blade and help keep the saw tracking true to the cut line. Note though: If the wood is wet, more kerf is needed to counteract the swelling of the wood around the blade due to friction heat.

WHICH ONES YOU NEED:

You'll want a pair of handsaws for use at a low, knee-height sawbench. Get a 5 to 6 tpi (teeth per inch) saw for ripping and an 8 tpi for crosscutting. If you will often be cutting thicker stock (6/4 and larger). The low sawbench and the long blades (26" to 28") allow you to make strokes to the full forward and backward motion of your arm, maximizing speed and efficiency. For sawing shorter (under 2') and thinner (under ¾") stock at the bench (you'll clamp the wood upright in a vise for ripping or hold it flat on the bench against a stop), you can go with shorter (20" to 24") panel saws with slightly finer teeth. Chose a rip at 7 tpi and a crosscut at 10 or 12 tpi. The shorter and finer-toothed saws are lighter and cut with less back pressure. They're easier to control when used standing upright at the bench because you don't have gravity and the larger muscles of your back that you gain at the sawbench.

Scrub and Cambered Blade Jack Plane

WHAT THEY DO:
You use a scrub plane or a jack plane fitted with a highly cambered blade to remove the "fuzz" on the surface of a rough-cut board and to reduce its thickness (usually by

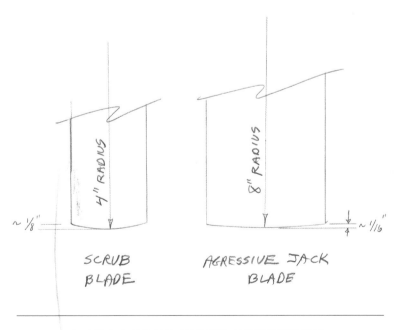

PLAN VIEW OF SCRUB PLANE AND CAMBERED JACKPLANE BLADES

pushing them directly across the grain of the board). You can also use these planes to narrow a board by running them along the edge of a board — though because of the coarseness of their cut, coupled with having an open mouth ahead of the blade, they can easily cause tear-out when cutting against the grain, causing you to remove material past your layout line.

HOW THEY DO IT:
The highly-curved blade of these planes makes them essentially a gouge. Every stroke creates a trough that can, in the case of the scrub plane, be ⅛" or more in depth. To reduce the thickness of the board, you simply plane a series of overlapping troughs across the width of the board, working from one edge to the other along the length of the board. It's energetic work (especially in dry hard woods), but you can get the surface of a rough sawn board ready for flattening and smoothing with bench planes surprisingly fast.

WHICH ONES YOU NEED:
If you intend to work with rough-cut lumber, then you will definitely want to have a scrub plane in your arsenal of handplanes. They come in two widths — get the narrower one if you are of small stature (under 150 pounds) as the narrower cut will be a little easier for you (with only a little loss of efficiency). If you are only occasionally going to surface a rough-faced board or if your lumber comes "skip-planed" (the fuzz is removed), you can opt out of the scrub plane and set up a jack plane with a dedicated scrubbing blade. You make the blade yourself by grinding (on a slow-turning grinder or a water wheel) an 8" to 10" radius curve on the cutting edge. You must move the frog back to open up the throat to pass the large shavings the blade will produce. If you are a larger person, consider going to a wider jack plane (#5½) to benefit by the added width of the blade and greater momentum of the heavier body.

Tools for Creating Planes and Angles — Bench Planes

The bench plane was, and still is, the signature tool of the artisan furnituremaker. It is the violin in the symphony of the tools of their trade, and it has been that way since the beginning of the craft of making useful objects from wood. There is probably no more distinctive or pleasant sound to the artisan's ear than the "snick" a sharp plane makes as it quickly sweeps across a board, lifting a perfectly even, tear-free shaving from the surface.

You use bench planes to produce what their name implies — a planar surface. They can make the face of the board dead flat and they can make the edges of the board dead straight and at whatever angle you want to the face. The standard bench planes are operated with two hands. Smaller versions for doing light-duty trimming can be used with one hand.

WHY AREN'T I SHOWING WOOD-BODIED BENCH PLANES?

There's nothing wrong with the traditional wood-bodied plane. In some (if not all) ways they are inherently superior to the metal plane: Their wood soles slide more freely on wood than does metal (which is why you have to constantly keep the metal soles lubricated with oil or wax throughout the planing process); the soles can be easily adjusted as necessary by the artisan to dead flat; their cutting irons are thick and more securely bedded to the plane body to prevent chatter and the blades are often set at a higher angle than most metal planes to enable them to deal with difficult wood. So why aren't I teaching to them? The short answer is: I trained with metal planes and know how to get the most out of them. I've used wooden planes (and I still use them for specialized tasks such as making moldings and sliding dovetails) but I've never learned to tune and use the bench versions to their full potential — so I'm not comfortable teaching to them. Plus, few students show up with a set of wooden planes these days!

Standard Bench Planes

WHAT THEY DO:

A bench plane, by lifting a uniformly thick slice of wood from the surface of the wood, imparts its own reference surface to the area being cut. If the sole of the plane is flat (and assuming you handle the tool properly), the wood left behind the blade will be flat as well. The longer the plane's sole, the more accurate the transfer happens over longer lengths of wood.

HOW THEY DO IT:

The plane is simply a jig for holding a chisel-like blade in a fixed relationship to the workpiece. As you run the plane along the board, the blade pares away the wood — but unlike a hand-guided chisel, the plane perfectly controls the depth of the cut for you. In modern iron-bodied planes, lever and screw mechanisms allow you to precisely set the blade's depth and to adjust it parallel to the base.

WHICH ONES YOU NEED:

In well-trained hands, you could probably emulate the late master furnituremaker Alan Peters and perform nearly all your bench plane work with a No. 7 jointer plane. If you go that route, I would suggest having a quiver of blades with a

Bench planes, from left-to-right: Lee Valley #5 bevel up with extra blades; Lie-Nielsen #8; Lie-Nielsen #5; and Lie-Nielsen #62.

variety of cambers and back bevels to change in and out as necessary. You could use blades with stronger cambers (with a more open throat setting) for removing coarse shavings; switch to a modest camber for light flattening and edge jointing work; and then to the shallowest camber (and tightest throat opening) for large-scale smoothing tasks. If you are dealing with difficult wood with a lot of reversing grain, you could drop in a blade with a back bevel of up to 15° to increase the cutting angle so it works more like a scraper and minimizes tear-out.

But if you've got the inclination (and the money), here's a list of the bench planes that you might want to keep on an open shelf near your planing bench and a description of the circumstances in which you would use them. The numbers refer to the industry standard, Stanley/Bailey numbering system. Note that I am not including dedicated smoothing planes in this section on bench planes, as their job is not to create planar surfaces but only to smooth them.

- **Jack plane (#5)**: General flattening and straightening work on smaller sized (up to 2' long) components.
- **Try plane (#8)**: A 2'-long plane for truing long edges straight and flattening the faces of larger boards and surfaces (such as bench and tabletops).
- **Low-angle jack plane (#62)**: A jack plane sized, low-angle plane for easily truing end grain. The low angle of the cutting edge (around 37°) severs the fibers exposed on end grain more easily and smoothly than does a standard 45° cutting angle (that angle is optimized for shearing — as opposed to severing — the tube-like fibers of the wood). On smaller stock, you'll often use this plane in conjunction with a shop-made shooting board to make precision trim cuts (as described in the next section of this book.)
- **Bevel-up Jack plane**: I offer this as an alternative to a standard jack plane and the #62 block plane. This type of plane gives you the ability to quickly drop in a steeper bevel blade to reduce tear-out when dealing with dense, contrary grain or to drop in a low-angle blade for truing end grain. The broad sidewalls of these planes also makes them suitable for use in a shooting board. The lack of a chipbreaker enables the change out to happen in about half the time it takes with a conventional plane.

Single-handed Block Planes

WHAT THEY DO:

Small-sized block planes (from 4" to 6" in length) are sized to fit in one hand for common tasks such as quickly trimming butt-type joints or making a light bevel along an edge. Finish carpenters love them because you can use the other hand to hold the wood either against your body or on top of a sawhorse. (You never see real woodworking benches on construction sites!) If you have a larger hand, you might also consider the smallest of the bench planes (such as the #3) as a one-handed plane — its greater mass makes it a little easier to use than a typical block plane on tougher woods or when making deeper cuts. You'll see me using this plane in the last project of this book.

HOW THEY DO IT:

These planes work the same way as all the other bench planes, but the blade is reduced in size so that the body of the plane can be made small enough to fit in one hand. Because the smaller-sized blade takes narrow (and usually shallow) cuts, the amount of effort required to work the plane is low enough for one-handed operation.

WHICH ONES YOU NEED:

Because much of the work these planes do often involves shaving end grain, it's best to choose a low-angle version. The bed angle of a low-angle block plane is usually 12°, which lifts the cutting angle of the bevel-up, 25° blade to 37°, considerably less than the standard 45° bench plane. The only downside is that the low-angle may cause tear-out — but you are almost never trying to smooth a surface with these planes. You can lessen the potential tear-out problem by keeping the blade sharp, reducing the opening ahead of the blade with the adjustable throat and backing off the blade to re-

Cluster of block planes, from left-to-right: Lie-Nielsen trimmer; Veritas block; and Lie-Nielsen block/rabbet.

duce the shaving thickness. Be cautious of the modern, imported versions of the Stanley 60½ — early versions of this tool were poorly engineered and machined. Instead, find an older Stanley or consider the contemporary interpretations from Lie-Nielsen, Lee Valley and later iterations of Stanley's premium "Sweetheart" line.

While you really need only one small block plane, you will eventually want to add a smaller and lighter version for doing common light work such as working a small bevel on the edge of a board to "break" the corner. They fit comfortably in the palm of your hand; in a small pouch of your work apron; and in your stocking by the fireplace at Christmas (hint).

Tools For Joinery: Chisels, Precision Saws and Specialty Joinery Planes

These are the tools that come into your hands once you have trued the boards to thickness, width and length. Though a large and diverse category, these tools share the common function of shaping the boards in ways that allow them to be joined together.

Chisels

WHAT THEY DO:

Chisels remove short lengths of the wood with either a paring or a chopping motion — most

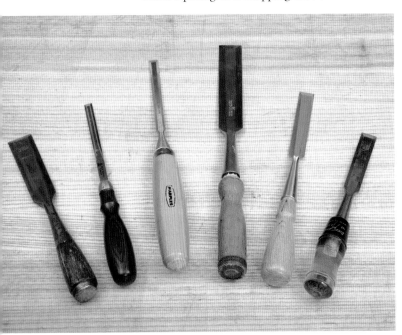

commonly in the creation of, and in the final fitting of, joints. When you need to chisel a longer section of wood — longer than what your hand motion or a tap from a mallet can provide — you put the chisel in a jig to help guide it. We call these jigs a plane!

HOW THEY DO IT:

The chisel is essentially a steel wedge that slices the fibers when used in a paring motion. (One hand provides the force while the other hand provides the brake and helps with directional control.) When impacted with a mallet, the wedge chops through the fibers (this strategy is used mostly across the grain). Chopping removes much thicker waste than paring — but with less fine control.

WHICH ONES YOU NEED:

For the majority of chisel work in traditional furniture making, you can get by with a set of bench chisels. They are thin enough for paring, but strong enough to stand up to a moderate amount of chopping. The side edges of a bench chisel are beveled to allow them to cut into angled corners. Get a set containing a range of sizes from ¼" to 1" in ⅛" increments. Fill in the ¹⁄₁₆" increments and get chisels larger than 1" as the need arises. If you find yourself often paring larger-sized joints, consider adding a wide and long-handled paring chisel. The wider blade does more work while the long handle gives you more leverage (torque) to do the work.

As your skills progress and you get into more refined or smaller-scale joinery, you'll want to add at least one or two thin chisels with shallow side bevels — to allow you to get into tight corners without marring the exposed edges of the joints. This is a common problem when doing narrow dovetails. You can modify a paring chisel to do the job by carefully grinding or filing shallow side bevels on a bench chisel, or you can buy dedicated dovetail or fishtail chisels. If you make really small joints, such as those in model making, you'll eventually want to add a set of very thin and narrow detail chisels.

If you decide to try your hand at making mortises entirely by hand using just a chisel (which is how they were almost always made by pre-industrial artisans), then you will need a really

A variety of bench chisels.

beefy chisel to hold up to the heavy chopping and leveraging. You won't need many — just one for each width of mortise you'll want to make. I have just two: a 5⁄16"-wide one for making mortises in ¾" stock and a 7⁄16" for 1⅛" stock — the two most common stock sizes in my work. If you really get into it, add a matching set of goose-necked chisels to make it easier to clean out the bottom of the mortise.

As you fall deeper into the rabbit hole of the world of hand tools, you'll likely be enticed by crank neck chisels. These are bench-style paring chisels with an offset blade to lift your hands up and away from the surface of the wood. They are handy for trimming plugs and through-mortises that land away from the edge of a board; and they are almost essential for chiseling out long dados. (You can use a router plane for this, but chiseling goes much faster — a router plane is really best used for final truing and flattening the bottom of the dado.)

While there is no end to the shapes and sizes of carving chisels (which is why we are going to leave the choice and use of them to other books) there is one curved-edge chisel that I think any traditional furnituremaker would find useful: a wide, shallow "firmer" gouge. You'll use this tool for many of the same tasks that a knife might be employed such as whittling the end of a peg to taper it — though with more comfort and control. You may also use the firmer gouge as a free-handed scrub plane to quickly remove, for example, the waste area of a board edge or a joint prior to final truing with a plane.

Dovetail; fishtail and set of detail chisels posed next to a run of dovetails.

Mortise and swan neck chisels posed next to a mortise.

Crank neck chisel posed next to a dado.

Shallow gouge removing waste in an end-rabbet.

Backsaws

WHAT THEY DO:

You'll use a backsaw mostly for making shallow, high-precision rips and crosscuts to create notches that will form a joint between two boards. You may also use it for cutting thin and narrow stock to precise length.

HOW THEY DO IT:

Backsaws are distinguished from standard handsaws (and the shorter panel saws) by a thick spine that runs along the edge of the blade opposite the teeth. The teeth are also generally much finer (they have much less work to do) and have little set — just enough to allow the blade to move without friction in the kerf made by the teeth. The spine stiffens the blade so it will track true to the intended cutline: The stiff blade self-references itself to its own kerf, which, having little set, prevents the saw from wandering in the cut. With a properly tuned backsaw, you will find that once you have started the cut accurately to the cutlines you can see, the saw tends to follow through almost on its own, cutting to the cutlines on the back of the board that you can't see!

A variety of backsaws.

WHICH ONES YOU NEED:

For smaller joinery such as dovetails and shallow (under 1") mortise and tenons, you can do fine with just one backsaw: a dovetail saw with 14 to 16 tpi configured for ripping. If you are doing small scale joinery, go with finer teeth up to 22 tpi — otherwise, you'll just sacrifice speed. Choose dovetail saws with a pistol-type grip instead of the straight handle. The latter is an ergonomic nightmare for your wrist and the round shaft gives your hand no feedback as to the position of the blade. You'll hold the pistol grip with three fingers, allowing your index finger to point alongside the handle — this grip instantly informs the relationship of the blade position to your hand, building muscle memory.

To saw out the larger joints typically involved in creating the framework of furniture pieces, you'll want to add a couple more backsaws to your stable: A crosscut, toothed carcase saw and a rip-filed tenon saw. Essentially, these are just larger and heavier versions of the dovetail saw that allow you to make deeper and wider cuts. While you could get away with just the carcase saw, you'll eventually want to add the tenon saw for faster cutting action when making cuts with the grain.

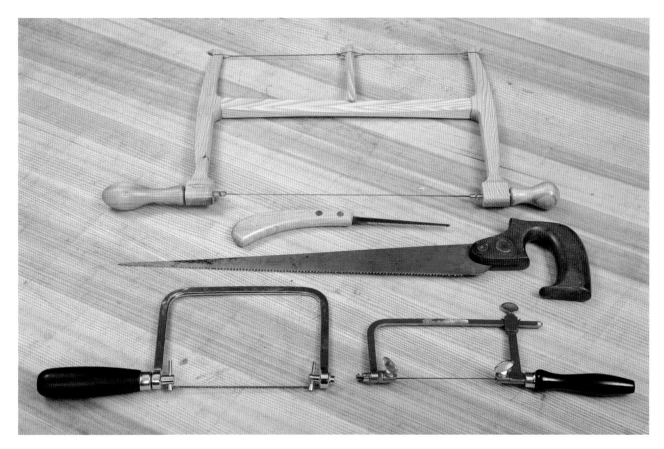

Specialty Saws

WHAT THEY DO:

When you want make a curved, rather than a straight, cut these are the saws you reach for. The coping saw (and the larger bow saw fitted with a narrow blade) will make cuts down to a radius of ⅛". Because keyhole, and the wider compass, saws have tapered blades, they don't do as good a job making a consistent curve. They are, however, the tool of choice for making a sawcut in the middle of a board (say for the sides of a long through-mortise or a handle-hole) — all you need do is give them a hole to start in. A sharp eyed reader may note that one of these saws, the keyhole saw, is actually a Japanese saw! I haven't found a source of good keyhole saws in the western sphere.

HOW THEY DO IT:

The narrow blades of the coping and bow saws do not self-reference to the kerfs they make — they are too narrow. Instead, these saws can turn in their kerf and go where you tell them to go. The lack of self-referencing, however, means they do not track well to the line, demanding constant attention and direction to cut accurately.

From top: a bow saw; keyhole saw; compass saw; and coping saws.

WHICH ONES YOU NEED:

For cutting curves (or cutting out the waste between dovetails) in thin (under ¾") stock, a coping saw is the perfect choice. A bow saw works well too and will give you more blade length and leverage for dealing with thicker stock. For joinery work you really only need the faster cutting, coarse-cutting blades (around 15 to 18 tpi) to cut away waste — you aren't trying to cut to a layout line. Switch to finer cut blades (20 tpi and higher) for cutting curves to a line in thin (under ½") stock (though you should still figure on trimming to the line with other tools). A keyhole saw will come in handy whenever you want to create slotted holes.

Specialty Joinery Planes

WHAT THEY DO:

The blades and soles of joinery planes are configured not to dimension, true or smooth the wood, but to create (or trim) a rectilinear shape in it. This shape can form an interlocking surface between two pieces of wood — in other words, a joint.

HOW THEY DO IT:

In all joinery planes, the sole of the tool is formed so that the shape of the blade is transferred into the wood. A rabbet plane — as well as the shoulder and the fancier fillister plane — allows the blade to cut right to the edge of the sole to form a crisp corner. Because the side of the sole is perpendicular to the base, the corner also forms a 90° angle. The plow plane is fitted with a narrow blade (you can choose different widths) and is configured to carry the blade away from the edge of the tool's fence — and therefore the edge of the board — so the blade can cut a groove. The router plane is configured to carry the blade away from the bottom of the plane — though the blade is still registered parallel to the sole. Because a frog doesn't back up the blade, however, it can vibrate and chatter easily — you don't want to use the router plane to create grooves on its own. Instead, use it mostly to clean up and true the bottom of an existing groove or other recessed surface such as a tenon cheek.

WHICH ONES YOU NEED:

The one specialty plane that I suggest you should own is a medium sized (with a ¾" blade) shoulder plane. You can use it for creating all manner of rabbets as well as trimming the shoulders and cheeks of tenons and other joints. You may never need another unless you get into doing larger (or much smaller) scale work.

A fancier version of the rabbet plane is the fillister plane. It adds a side fence and a depth stop, and some versions feature a skewed blade that eases cross-grain cutting as well as helping to pull the plane into the wood (which keeps the fence registered against the edge.) Another feature of fillister planes is the inclusion of a spur cutter ahead of the blade to pre-cut the wood when planing across the grain to prevent tear-out. These planes are available in right- and left-hand configurations (not for your handedness, but to allow you to choose the plane that will go with the grain of the wood along an edge). If your projects start calling for a lot of rabbet work, then a fillister plane (a pair is nice but not really necessary) will start calling to you.

The other specialty plane that may soon demand your attention (especially for making drawers and door frames) is the plow plane. When you are ready to give up making grooves with your router or table saw (or you don't want to go there to begin with), then you'll want a plow plane and a set of blades. Like the fillister (and for the same reason) the plow planes are available in right- and left-hand versions. I suggest first going with the basic plow plane rather than the far more complex versions called combination planes (such as the Stanley 45 and 55) that feature double skates (thin soles) to allow them to cut beads and wider grooves.

Other specialty planes that you may want to add to your tool box include a small shoulder plane (mostly for trimming the end-grain shoulders of a joint and making small fitting rabbets); a router plane for cleaning out dados and precisely truing tenon cheeks and lap joints; an edging plane for truing an edge or end of a board to its face, and, more for fun than anything, a combination tongue-and-groove plane that can make a groove in one board and a matching tongue in the other by just changing the position of its guide fence.

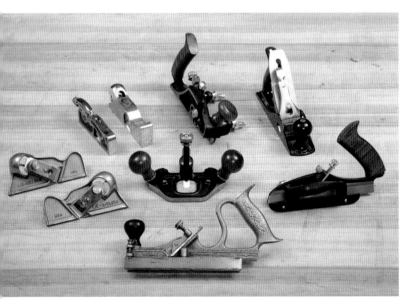

A grouping of joinery planes: rabbet, fillister, router, plow, shoulder, edge-trimming, and tongue-and-groove.

Tools for Shaping Edges: Drawknives & Spokeshaves

WHAT THEY DO:

The drawknife can remove extremely coarse shavings along the length of a board, bringing it quickly down to a cutline. You can also use the tool to impart a changing curve with, or across, the grain by varying the thickness of the shaving to create decorative chamfers. Unlike most other Western-style tools, and contrary to the most fundamental safety rule in hand tool woodworking, you always pull the drawknife toward you. (It's safe, however, because it's essentially impossible to pull your arms back far enough for the blade to touch your chest.)

The spokeshave, with a sole surrounding the blade to control the depth of cut, removes fine shavings and is often used to remove the facets left behind by the coarser cutting drawknife. It may be pushed or pulled. The small sole of the spokeshave is shaped flat or to a curve fore and aft of the blade — the latter allows the tool to work along the inside of a concave edge. Another type of spokeshave features a sole curved across the width of a similarly curved blade, either convex or concave — this feature, most useful in chairmaking, help you smooth cylinders or channels produced by coarser tools.

HOW THEY DO IT:

Drawknives are essentially two-handed paring chisels. Because you can use both hands, you can impart a tremendous amount of power to the cutting edge as you pull the tool toward you with the large muscles of your back. The short length of the blade (unlike the long blade of a paring chisel) allows you to maintain a considerable amount of control over the depth and direction of the cut. For coarse cutting, you apply the drawknife bevel up to the wood; for more controllable, finer cuts, you put the bevel down.

WHICH ONES YOU NEED:

Start with an 8"-wide drawknife — be sure the bevel is ground at a low (20° to 30°) angle. (Some contemporary versions have steep, 45° bevels and are much harder to pull through the dry hardwoods encountered in furniture making — they are probably optimized for working with green wood and paring off bark.) For doing light-duty chamfering, you may want to acquire

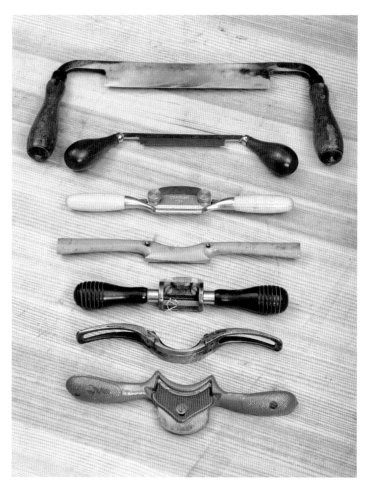

Drawknives, large and small, at top, and a selection of spokeshaves.

a smaller, lighter and easier to handle 4" blade-width drawknife.

Unless you are doing a lot of work with cylindrical shapes (think: "chairmaking") you can probably go your whole life without the curved blade spokeshaves. You will, however, want at least one spokeshave for cleaning up after the drawknife and other coarse cutting tools. You can choose from the traditional wood-bodied, low-angle (bevel-up) variety or from the steeper-pitched metal body types. I find the former much easier to use and less prone to chatter, though not as easy to sharpen as the latter. You'll want two: a curved sole so you can smooth inside curves and a flat sole version for dealing with outside curves.

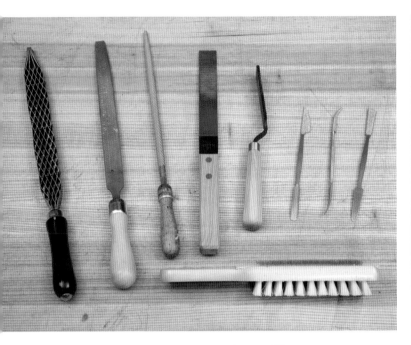

Rasps and Rifflers

WHAT THEY DO:

Rasps, rifflers and floats aggressively, but controllably, encourage the wood to take the shape of the tool's cutting surface. A curved rasp will create a channel of the same radius, for example. Relative to using a gouge, there is less chance of tear-out because the cutters of this category of tool are so small they act more like a scraper than a chisel — they simply can't cut very deep. These tools are often used for quickly creating complex shapes along the edges of a board when creating sculpted joints or for simply wasting away wood to create a rounded corner. Floats are a specialized version of a rasp and are mostly used for flattening and truing hard-to-reach areas such as the inside walls of a mortise.

HOW THEY DO IT:

The rasp is essentially a steel plate studded with a multitude of tiny teeth that act like miniature chisels as they are drawn or pushed over the wood. (Floats are different; their teeth are shaped more like knives as they span the full width of the plate — and, unlike a rasp they can be resharpened by using a triangular file.) Whatever shape the steel plate is, so will be the shape it imparts to the wood.

WHICH ONES YOU NEED:

For most typical furniture work, you can get away with just one rasp: A patternmaker's rasp

featuring a flat surface on one side of the plate and a curve on the other. The Nicholson #50 is typical and a perfect one to start with. You can add the coarser #49 if you want to speed things up a bit. Rasps made by Auriou feature hand-cut teeth and, because of their higher level of performance, are the gold standard for rasps. Japanese steel mesh rasps are another alternative that work well. If you are going to do any sculptural work involving fine detail work, you will want to acquire a basic set of rifflers, adding more as the need arises.

Gouges

Gouges are curved-shaped chisels that create channels of various widths and radii — and are therefore essential to carving shapes in the wood. There are a seemingly infinite variety of gouges to choose from, though I've found that the more experienced the carver, the fewer tools they use. While the choice and use of gouges is far beyond the scope of this book on setting up a hand tool shop, I can assure you that gouges will eventually become an essential part of your tool kit as you move into doing decorative details, traditional carvings or contemporary sculptural work on your furniture projects.

WHICH ONES YOU NEED:

For furniture work you will generally want to avoid the smaller, "palm" sized chisels intended for small-scale relief or chip carving. Instead, select the larger sized chisels with full-sized handles. A basic set will include a selection of curves and at least one V-shaped "veiner" for outlining work.

Molding Planes and Scratch Stock

WHAT THEY DO:
You use molding planes to create decorative shapes along the edge of a board. (If you rip off the shape from the board, you will have created a molding that can be applied in a variety of ways to the piece of furniture.) A scratch stock does the same, but at a much smaller scale — sometimes to make a simple decorative bead or to create a groove for an inlay. A scratch stock can be used along a curved as it registers its narrow face to the edge of the board.

HOW THEY DO IT:
Molding planes are just like any other plane — they carry a chisel across the wood, imparting the shape of the blade and sole to the surface below. Unlike bench planes, however, the chisel and sole of molding planes are not flat and therefore the shape being transferred to the wood is not flat either — instead it is a hollow, a round or a combination of both. Like carving tools, there is almost an infinite number of shapes that can be created. A scratch stock works more like a scraper, carrying a small, shaped blade at a high angle into the wood. You work the shape by drawing an overlapping series of short strokes rather than planing a continuous shaving.

WHICH ONES YOU NEED:
One approach is to pick up random antique molding planes as they show up in sales online and elsewhere. That does mean, however, that you will be designing to the tools you own for

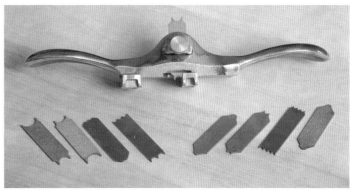

a while. It also usually means dealing with restoring a tool to working order — and molding planes are notorious for warped soles and abused or over-used blades. Another, and perhaps better, approach is to decide what kind of moldings you want to make and then purchase a new hollow and round set to make that molding. You can find both domestic and imported sources for these tools (see the Resources on page 175).

DIY SCRATCH STOCK

Most woodworking tool suppliers carry scratch stocks and sets of blades to go with them. You can also very easily make your own scratch stock by shaping a bit of old hand saw blade with a file and then capturing the blade in a wooden block. Garrett Hack teaches how to do this in classes that he offers all around the country.

Vermont cabinetmaker and author Garrett Hack with his shop-made scratch stock.

Tools for Smoothing the Wood — Precision Shearing Tools

Once you learn to get a bench plane working to its full potential, you will discover that you almost never have to sand a wood surface to make it smooth. Instead, a short plane optimized for smoothing will shear off gossamer-thin shavings, leaving behind a mirror-like sheen. (It actually is a mirror when viewed from a low angle.) In the instance where the smooth plane causes a bit of tear-out, you can come back with a scraper to smooth that area. Files clean up the curved, rough surfaces left behind by rasps while fine-grit sandpaper (220 and up) smoothes curved edges to remove the tool marks (facets) left behind by chisels and planes. It might be helpful to remember that in artisan-era woodworking, such tool marks were rarely removed — so that last step is really a style-driven option.

Smoothing Planes

WHAT THEY DO:
A smoothing plane is a bench plane — usually the #4 size at 9" to 10" long — that has been optimized to cut very thin shavings with a minimum of tear-out. Its job isn't to surface the wood flat, it's just to make it smooth and ready for finishing.

An infill-type smoothing plane made from a Ron Brese kit by Nole Pritchard.

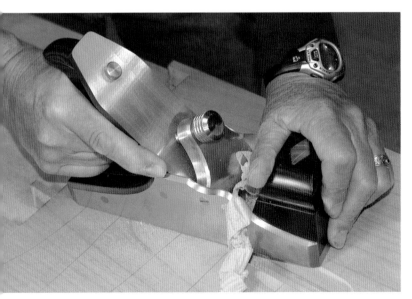

HOW THEY DO IT:
Any plane will take fine shavings if you are working with a sharp edge; you back out the blade to take a shallow cut; and you are careful to never plane against the grain — which may be impossible in some situations. To prevent any potential for tear-out, however, a dedicated smooth plane is specifically optimized for that task. (This is important because tear-out is a real setback when the wood has been dimensioned to a certain thickness and there is no margin for taking off more material).

A very tight throat opening ahead of the blade (no more than three times the thickness of the shavings being cut), provides pressure just ahead of the cutting action, holding the wood down so that the blade can shear it cleanly from the surface. Without that tightly spaced pressure, the wood might shear below the surface before it breaks away, creating a tear in the surface. This is also why dedicated metal smoothing planes tend to be heavier than similar-sized bench planes — the weight helps maintain that pressure ahead of the blade. To prevent vibration (which produces chatter marks in the wood) a modern dedicated smooth plane will feature a blade at least twice as thick as a standard bench plane blade and it will be precisely seated and securely held against a very solid frog to prevent any rocking movement. The cutting edge of a smooth plane's blade should be either gently curved or the corners rounded so that the troughs left behind the plane show no ridges at their edges.

WHICH ONES YOU NEED:
At first, you can easily get away with optimizing a standard #4-sized bench plane to do the job of smoothing. Just be sure that the sole of the plane is dead flat, that the blade is very sharp and slightly cambered (just a few thousandths of an inch rise toward either side), and that the frog is sitting securely on the sole. Check to be sure the blade doesn't rock on the face of the frog. Finally, close up the mouth by moving the frog forward. You now have a smoothing plane that will lift gossamer shavings on most wood surfaces, though you must be sure to go with the grain of the wood as much as possible. If you do expect to encounter opposing grain, you can raise the blade's "angle of attack" by honing a back bevel of up to 15° on the face of the blade (see "Sharpening" on page 64). This trick enables the blade to meet the wood at a high angle, encouraging it

Smoothing planes: At top, an Ulmia wood body. From left at bottom, Lee Valley bevel-up #4, Lie-Nielsen #4½ bevel up, and a Stanley #3.

to break the fibers more quickly from the surface before they have a chance to dive beneath.

If you want to really get into it (there is no bottom to this rabbit hole), only your pocketbook will stop you! For dealing with more difficult woods such as curly maple (or, for that matter, any board that has changing grain on the same surface), you will eventually want to get the "real" thing: a dedicated smoothing plane. The best of the best are the infill planes which are machined to very high tolerances, are extremely heavy for their size, have very thick blades, and have beds (NOTE: frogs are movable bits) that hold the blades at a higher-than-normal angle of attack. (The standard bench plane's frog face is 45° relative to the sole). You can find antique infill planes (Norris was a common brand) or you can find versions made by contemporary plane makers such as the large smoother by Ron Brese as shown in the photo at the far left. (His contact information is listed in the Resources.) Another choice for premium smooth planes are the older Stanley #4 planes and the Lie-Nielsen upgraded versions of the Bed Rock which are available with steeper frogs, higher construction tolerances and thicker blades and cap irons.

Another type of dedicated smooth plane you might consider (an excellent version is available from Lee Valley) features an extremely thick bevel-up blade. The thickness of the blade precludes the need for a chipbreaker (also making the blade faster to remove from the plane for honing) and, because it's the bevel of the blade that meets the wood, you can easily adjust the plane to meet the wood at a higher angle of attack by simply switching out the blade for one with a steeper bevel. For smoothing end grain, you could install a low-angle (25°) blade.

A final note: You may notice that many smoothing planes, including the Lee Valley bevel-up version and most of the infill types, lack flat sidewalls on the sides of the sole. This configuration isn't necessary because dedicated smoothing planes are not meant to be laid on their sides to shoot the end of a board. They cut too slowly, for one thing; and the high cutting angles make them hard to push across end grain.

Scrapers

WHAT THEY DO:

Scrapers (which is, by the way, a misnomer since the tool doesn't actually scrape the wood unless it's dull) are nothing more than a piece of high-carbon steel with a cutting edge — usually a burr — worked into its thin edge. This edge, when pushed across the surface of the wood, removes very thin shavings with virtually no visible tear-out.

HOW THEY DO IT:

Because the blade of a scraper instantly meets the wood at a very high angle (always forward of 90°) just behind the burr cutting edge, it becomes physically impossible for the cut to dive below the surface of the wood to cause tear-out. While this also severely limits the thickness and length of the shavings, it does ensure that this tool will surface the wood without producing defects no matter what direction the grain is running. You make the burr by rolling the sharpened edge with a hardened steel burnisher.

WHICH ONES YOU NEED:

Because you will likely use the scraper only as a follow up to the smoothing plane where necessary — to perhaps follow rasps on curved parts, or to occasionally remove glue squeeze-out — you can get away with just a single thin card scraper that you'll guide with your hands. You can vary the depth of cut by just pressing on the back of the blade to flex in a curve. (Be sure to wear gloves, though — friction makes these blades extremely hot!) There are holders for these blades, including plane-like bodies, but I have rarely found the need for them. If your work includes making sculpted surfaces (such as carved legs), then you will want to add some "gooseneck" shaped scrapers to your arsenal.

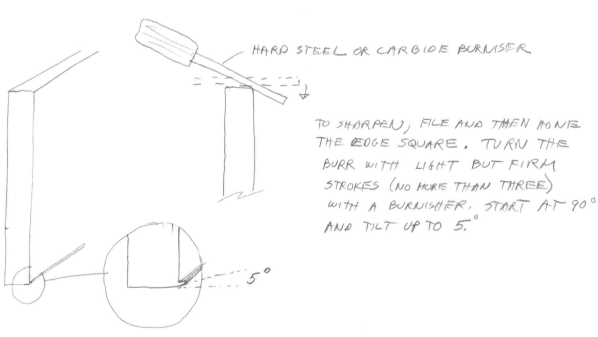

HARD STEEL OR CARBIDE BURNISER

TO SHARPEN, FILE AND THEN HONE THE EDGE SQUARE. TURN THE BURR WITH LIGHT BUT FIRM STROKES (NO MORE THAN THREE) WITH A BURNISHER. START AT 90° AND TILT UP TO 5.°

5°

PUTTING A BURR ON A SCRAPER BLADE

Files

WHAT THEY DO:
Files cleanly remove wood to mimic the shape of the file's cutting surface. You will commonly use them to smooth the shaped surfaces left behind by the coarser rasps or chisels. You'll use a triangular file for shaping and honing saws … these will be covered later.

HOW THEY DO IT:
The scored surface of the file makes it act as if it were a closed, grouped stack of scraper blades, removing fine shavings with almost no incidence of tear-out to the wood fibers. The finer the file, the finer the shavings and the smoother the surface left behind.

WHICH ONES YOU NEED:
Unless you are doing a lot of sculpted work, you can get away with a single cabinetmaker's file (which has one flat and one curved surface) and a round file. If you are sculpting, you will want a set of riffler files that include all manner of curves and shapes.

Sanding Tools

WHAT THEY DO:
Sandpaper, composed of tiny grits of abrasive material, scrapes away the wood. The finer the grit, the smaller the scratches it produces and the smoother the surface feels to the touch. Held against a shaped block, the paper will mimic in the wood the shape of the surface backing it.

HOW THEY DO IT:
Tiny minerals in crystalline form are bonded to a paper substrate. When rubbed over a softer surface (such as wood), the crystals tear away the material, leaving behind a mesh of scratches. If the scratches are tiny and run with the grain of the wood, they are difficult to detect.

WHICH ONES YOU NEED:
Keep a selection of grits from 120 to 400 on hand — the variety available in rolls with a self-adhesive backing is the most useful. Your can cut off a piece and fold it over on itself to make it stiffer for holding in your hand, or apply the piece to a sanding block. You will want a wide selection of blocks: a soft, foam-like block for sanding surfaces with changing planes and curves;

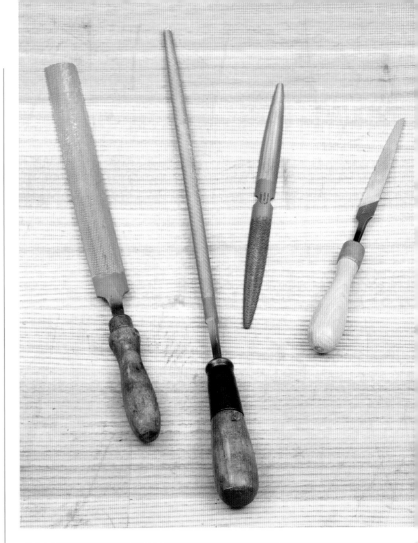

a stiff, flat block for smoothing a flat surface, and a selection of stiff foam blocks that you can carve to any shape necessary.

Tools For Making Holes: Bit Turning Tools

I suppose you could make a round hole in wood by pounding away with a rounded chisel (such as a gouge with an inside bevel) — but you would soon wish someone would invent a chisel that would turn in a circle, shearing a perfectly sized hole as deep as you wanted to go while removing the shavings and then stopping precisely when you wanted to stop. Lucky for us, someone many centuries ago did just that and called it a brace and auger. In traditional furniture making, there are now numerous types of drill bits and their hand-powered drivers to choose from based on the size and speed of the hole you want to produce.

Brace and Bits

WHAT THEY DO:
The brace, set up with an appropriate sized bit, produces a hole of a precise diameter in or through the wood. The brace allows you to exert far more force than you can via a geared, "egg-beater"-type drill and is therefore the tool of choice for drilling holes ¼" or larger. You'll use the brace often for drilling shaft and pilot holes for larger fasteners, making countersinks for the head of a screw and for removing waste in certain joints

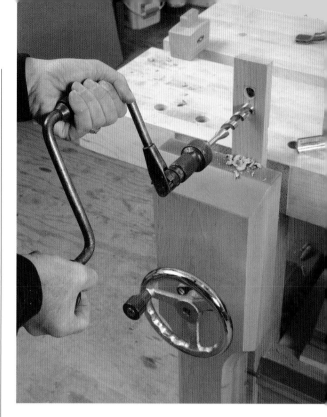

(such as mortises and stopped dados). While not a typical use in furnituremaking, carpenters and boatbuilders often used the brace as an extremely powerful driver for large screws and lagbolts.

HOW THEY DO IT:
The brace is a crank — a lever that provides a powerful rotational force to the cutting edge of a bit as it shears the fibers. The larger the hole you want to make, the wider you want the crank on the brace to be in order to gain leverage (because torque is measured in foot-pounds). To go faster, when drilling small holes, choose a narrower brace. The auger bits, having flutes running along the length of most of their shaft at the dimension of the hole being made, self-reference the bit and to help keep the hole going straight. The flutes are also an inclined plane in the reverse direction of the cutting rotation to carry the cut-off chips up and out of the hole, reducing clogging. (This is a good reason, by the way, to lubricate the fluted shaft of auger bits with wax or oil.) A lead screw at the center of the bit and ahead of the cutters helps draw the bit into the wood and keeps the cutters engaged.

WHICH ONES YOU NEED:
For most traditional furniture making, you can probably get away with just one brace — one with a 10" wide sweep. It may not be as easy to use as the largest size braces (12" to 14" sweeps) when drilling holes larger than 1" in diameter,

Brace and bits; three sizes of brace are shown, along with auger bits, center bits and drivers.

Countersink bits — brace type and handle type.

but it will be faster when drilling holes under 1"! (Power through leverage comes with a sacrifice: speed). If you are going to be drilling larger holes in your projects (or driving large fasteners), then you will definitely want the largest brace you can find. For quickly drilling countersink holes for screws, go with an 8" wide sweep.

There are a few things to know about auger bits: One type (Irwin) has flutes that wrap around a thick inner shaft while a second type (Jennings) has no inner shaft at all — the flutes are configured like an unsupported spiral staircase. Because the sides of the flutes of this latter type are broad, the bit contributes enormously toward keeping the hole going straight. The downside, however, is these bits are not as strong as the center shaft variety and can bend when overstressed. They also tend to clog more than other types. Choose the Irwin shaft-type if you are commonly drilling into dense hardwoods such as oak and maple. You'll want a set that ranges in sixteenths of an inch from ¼" to 1" in diameter. Buy larger sizes as you need them.

Finally, take a close look at the lead screw of the auger. Some are fine threaded (optimized for drilling into endgrain or dense wood because it slows down the cutting action to make the bit easier to turn) while others are quite coarse. I find that the fine threaded ones generally clog too easily, losing their grip and then ceasing to help draw the bit into the wood. If you have a choice, go with the medium- or coarse-threaded leads.

When drilling shallow holes or holes through thin wood where you don't need the help of an auger bit to ensure a long, straight hole, you can choose to use the less expensive, easier to sharpen center bit. Avoid using them when the hole needs to be more than ¾" or so deep as the shallow cutter and thin shaft invariably allows the hole to wander, going off your intended course. You can also use standard Forstner and spade-type bits in a brace for making shallow holes.

Finally, if you are going to be drilling holes in green wood, especially at an angle (a common task in traditional chairmaking) then you will need the specialized spoon bits. These are still made and available at outlets such as Lee Valley or Woodcraft.

Different types of auger, center and spoon bits.

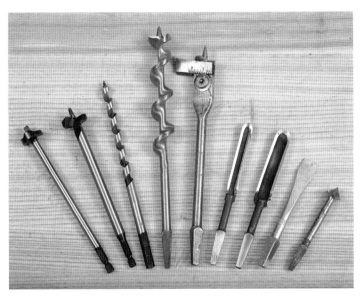

Push and Crank Drills

WHAT THEY DO:

These hand-powered drills produce little leverage but turn quickly and are therefore useful for making smaller holes (less than ¼"). In traditional furniture making, you'll use them mostly for drilling pilot holes for fastenings.

HOW THEY DO IT:

The push drill works through the magic of the inclined plane. When you push on the handle, it runs down a long screw and converts the pushing movement into a rotational one, turning the bit. The fluted bits that are often supplied with the push drills are designed to cut when turned in either direction, speeding up the process. The egg beater drills use standard twist drills.

WHICH ONES YOU NEED:

You will want a push drill for the oft called-upon task of making pilot holes for nails. Be sure the drill has its own set of bits — most push drills won't accept standard drill bits and can be proprietary to a certain attachment mechanism. For the somewhat larger holes required by screws, choose a standard sized eggbeater — though I've come to prefer to use a brace with a small sweep. It turns nearly as fast and doesn't have the eggbeaters annoying habit of jamming or pinching fingers. My preference, though, is to install driver bits into my smallest sweep (8") brace. The small sweep creates high rpm at the bit (although with less power than a larger sweep).

Push and eggbeater drills and drill bits.

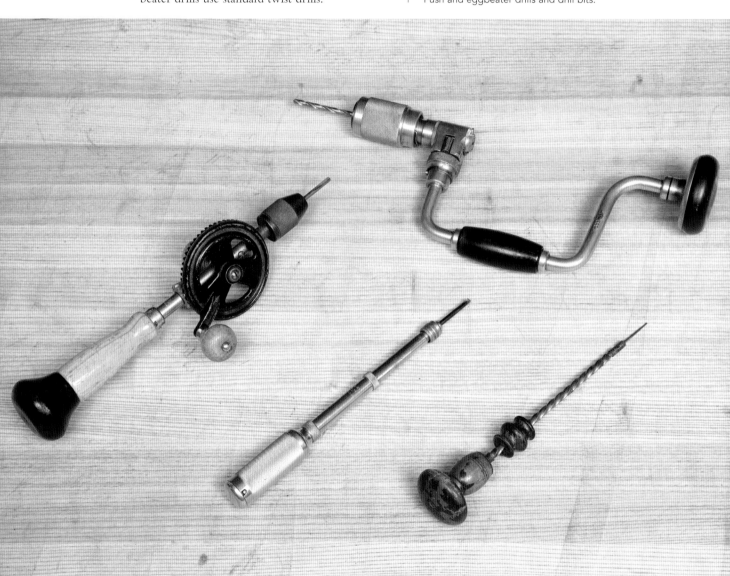

Hand-twisted Drills

WHAT THEY DO:

In softer furniture woods such as sugar pine or alder, you don't necessarily have to drill a through pilot hole for a fastener to prevent it from splitting the wood. Often, just a starting hole will do the trick, and the bradawl does this for you with just a couple twists of your wrist. The gimlet creates a threaded hole the same width and length as the screw it was designed to match.

HOW THEY DO IT:

The bradawl (not to be confused with a regular awl) is actually a miniature chisel — either in the shape of a triangle or of a very thin and sharp screwdriver blade. When you twist and untwist the tool, the point cuts a little hole in the wood. You need only go in an ⅛" or so to create a starting point for a screw or nail. The gimlet is simply a tap for a screw — the tip of this tool is nothing more than a screw with sharp, deep threads. A flute along the shaft carries shavings out of the cut, allowing you to drill as deep as the screw requires. It's slow going, but it works.

WHICH ONES YOU NEED:

One bradawl is all you'll ever need for starting small nails and tiny screws. Gimlets come in sets so they can handle the full range of screws used in typical furniture projects. They work well, but are slow, as they must be twisted out at the same (slow) speed they went in. They are probably the reason cordless drills were invented!

Tools for Assembling Parts

The assembly process in hand tool woodworking is fundamentally different than what's generally encountered in machine tool woodworking. In the latter, all the parts are precut to dimension including, in most cases, all the male and female portions of all the joints. If the machines were properly calibrated and nothing went awry during processing (which is, after all, the goal and the whole point of machining, rather than working the wood), all the pieces will come together at once in the final assembly. This is how, in today's industrial economy, you make money when your goal is do woodworking for a living.

In pre-industrial, hand tool woodworking, however, the assembly process was radically different (though they were, of course, still motivated to make a living!). In its purest form, the artisan dimensioned each piece of the project individually, deriving its final width, thickness and/or length from the piece to which it would be attached. When he made a joint such as tenon or a dovetail, he traced them to produce their mating socket. Each piece, then, was fit to the next. A series of mini-assemblies instead of a global assembly performed at the end of a manufacturing process that precut all the parts to size. While most of the tools for assembly are essentially the same for either approach (unless we include hydraulic clamping machines!), this little treatise serves as a heads-up to prepare you for how we will be assembling the shop projects presented in the second section of this book.

Hammers and Mallets

WHAT THEY DO:

A hammer or mallet turns your hand into a far more powerful and concentrated impact tool than the palm of your hand alone could provide. A hammer features a metal head, which has the required density for driving a metal fastening into the wood. A mallet with a wood or dense plastic head is used to encourage wood to overcome the friction within the mating surface of its joints so the pieces fit tightly together. I also use the plastic-headed hammer for driving rose-headed, copper nails to prevent putting unsightly dents in the "rose."

HOW THEY DO IT:

The head of the mallet provides the mass for moving things while the handle provides the head with leverage — the longer the handle, the more the foot-pounds exerted on impact. Be aware, though, that the longer the handle, the harder it becomes to aim accurately (that's why most people choke up on the handle of hammers when driving small nails). Heavier heads also add to the impact, of course. The more mass you have to move, the heavier (and usually larger) mallet or hammer you will need to use.

WHICH ONES YOU NEED:

For making furniture you generally need only a couple of hammers: a 13-ounce standard claw hammer for driving small nails and a lighter "Warrington"-style tack hammer for driving tacks and brads. Likewise, you can get away with just two mallets: A small, lightweight mallet for such tasks as tapping on the head of a chisel when chopping away at the cross-grain base line of small joints such as dovetails; and a larger, heavier mallet with a longer handle for heavy chopping (as often encountered in making mortises) and for encouraging larger

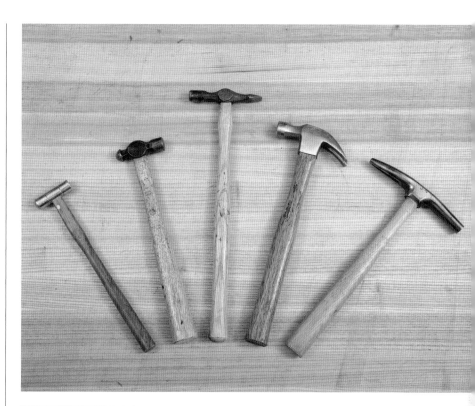

pieces of wood to come together. In the latter case, however, you nearly always have to provide some sort of buffer (such as a piece of softwood) between the mallet head and the wood being beat upon to prevent marring. To avoid that hassle, consider adding a rubber-headed mallet to your collection of beaters.

Clamps

WHAT THEY DO:

Because proper and thorough clamping is often critical to the accurate and efficient assembly of components and long laminations — and because you should never, ever ask fasteners to draw parts together — the old saw that says "you can't have more than enough clamps" happens to be true. Clamps also pull parts together with a much steadier and controlled force than does the brute force of a mallet's impact and they continue to hold the parts together while you add fastenings or wait for glue to dry.

So why shouldn't you use fastenings instead of a bunch of clamps to pull parts or boards together? The answer is that while the fasteners might exert enough force to do the job, they are doing so at the expense of their holding power over time. This is because the threads — which are nothing more than very narrow grooves in the wood — may have been severely stressed and weakened by the tension you placed upon them. Screws really aren't for drawing things together; they are for holding things together.

HOW THEY DO IT:

Clamps generally work by squeezing a workpiece between two points: one fixed and one moving. The moving piece exerts its force through either a screw mechanism (which in physics would be called an inclined plane) or by some form of wedge (which is the physics behind most sliding "squeeze" clamps) — or sometimes a combination of both as featured in "F"-style clamps. All metal screw-type clamps (mostly "C"-clamps) are capable of exerting the most force (which is why large versions are popular in boat yards where they are often asked to edge-set thick planks prior to fastening them to frames). Note: In furniture construction, you should never require much force to draw any components together — if it takes the force of an inclined plane, you should retreat and see what's going wrong and fix the problem by trimming the offending areas rather than overcoming them through brute force.

WHICH ONES YOU NEED:

Unless you are building a boat, you really don't need that many clamps to build most traditional-style furniture projects. (Furniture with veneers and laminated curved components is another matter.) You can get away with as little as two or three bar (or the cheaper pipe) clamps as long as the bars are longer than the largest assembly you think you will ever be dealing with. A few small wood-jawed clamps are handy for squeezing small frame joints such as laps and bridles together and holding them while the glue dries. Two pairs of 2' long, F-style clamps will draw and hold a drawer together. The more joints or drawers you build prior to assembly, the more pairs of clamps you'll want to have on hand for the sake of efficiency.

Fasteners

WHAT THEY DO:

Furniture makers call on fasteners to hold various pieces of a project together where physical interlocks (we call them joints) are impractical or impossible. Common applications are to use small nails to attach lightweight parts such as moldings; larger nails to hold larger surfaces in place (such as a panel board to the rabbet of a framework); and screws to hold pieces in place that might be subject to a lot of load (such as drawer runners). Rarely, a furniture maker may have to employ a carriage bolt when building larger structures that may need to be knocked down for transport. The carriage bolt is also the strongest fastener relative to nails and screws. As a general rule, the faster the fitting installs, the less fast the fitting.

To install the screws, I call on a variety of hand-powered drivers: From a 10" to 14" brace for larger (thicker) fasteners, to "Yankee" type ratcheting drills that covert your pushing action into a rotation at the driver, to standard screwdrivers.

HOW THEY DO IT:

Metal fasteners take the form of either an inclined plane (a screw) or a wedge (a nail). The screw winds its way into the wood along a pre-drilled pilot hole traveling through one piece and into another. The head of the screw acts as a stop to keep the first part pressed against the second part. The immense friction of the threads resists any forces working to back it out. (If you are concerned about the strength of the screw fastening, you will want to pre-thread the pilot hole so the screw threads don't have to — more on that later). A nail also holds itself in place with friction, pulling the piece it passes through against the underlying piece — though with less inertia than a screw. Rectangular cross-section nails (called cut nails) chop their way into the wood instead of simply forcing the fibers apart as round nails do. This characteristic tends to reducing splitting and helps the nail hold better. Carriage bolts don't rely on friction with wood to hold the pieces or stay in place — instead a nut threads onto the bolt and bears against the outside surface of the underlying piece.

WHICH ONES YOU NEED:

On the following page is a list of the most commonly used fasteners for typical, traditional furniture making. Note that you should choose screws

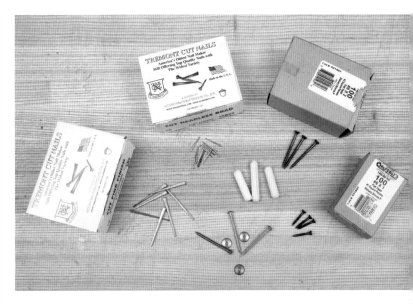

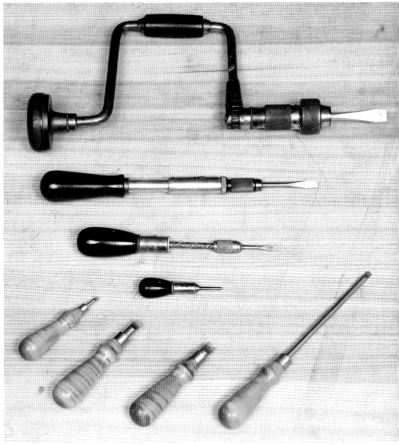

that are engineered specifically for fastening wood (avoid sheetrock screws — they are far too brittle and thin). For nails, I prefer the strength of cut nails over round wire nails. Cut nails also don't always need pilot screws to prevent splitting because the cutting action of their chisel-shaped cross section. Sources for these fasteners are listed in the Resources section.

FASTENERS FOR TRADITIONAL FURNITURE MAKING

NAILS:

"Square"- Shank Cut Nails (From Tremont Nail Co.)
- 7/8" Cut Headless Brad — For attaching moldings
- 1½" Cut Fine Finish — For structural fastening
- 2" Cut Fine Finish — For structural fastening

Copper Nails, "Rose"- Head
- 13 and 12 Gauge, Various Lengths — Decorative, light-duty fastening.

Escutcheon Pins
- Various Sizes and Gauges — Decorative attachment of moldings; pins for sector.

SCREWS:
- Brass Flat and Oval Head — Hardware attachment; also use on shop fixtures where fasteners may come in contact with cutting edges.
- Flat-Head, Square Drive Wood Screws — Used for high load, structural attachment. Choose statuary bronze-plated finish, if heads exposed, for moderate corrosion resistance and appearance. (#6 - ½" to 1"; #8 - 1¼" to 2½")
- Pocket Hole Screws — Choose round washer-head, square drive for more holding power.

Glues

WHAT THEY DO:
Unless you are attaching veneers to a substrate, a woodworker building traditional furniture can almost get away without using glue at all! Certain joints such as laps (and, to a lesser extent, dovetails) do require glue to prevent them from moving in a direction not contained by their interlocking structure. Mortise-and-tenon joints that are either locked in place with offset pegs (called "drawbored") or with wedges do not require glue to hold them in place. In most traditional furnituremaking, glue is used to prevent slippage, never to add strength.

HOW THEY DO IT:
Glues use the chemistry of a liquid turning to a solid to lock wood fibers together. While the glue is in liquid form, it penetrates into the wood, flowing around and sometimes into the fibers. Through the magic of chemistry, when the glue is thin it gets the message that it should turn from a liquid into a solid. When that happens it forms a rigid matrix across the gap between the boards, locking around the surrounding longitudinal, tubular fibers.

WHICH ONES YOU NEED:
For furniture making, you can almost get away with one type of glue: Either traditional hide glue (available today in liquid form so you don't have to melt flakes in a glue pot!) or any one of the "yellow," water-soluble carpenter's wood glues. You can opt for a waterproof variety of the latter if you feel the furniture is going to be exposed to excessively moist conditions. You might, for example, go this route if you were building a table for kids to do crafts at.

If you are going to get fancy and apply veneers, the glue of choice is warmed up, liquid hide glue. You could use the carpenter's glues, but you you'll have a more difficult time removing that veneer for patching or replacing. The hide glue more readily gives up the ghost when it encounters hot water or steam.

The only other glue you might want to keep on hand is a small tube of "super-glue" (which is nothing more than plastic in liquid form) for wicking into, and instantly repairing, a raised splinter. If you are allergic to these glues (and many people are), you can simply inject thinned carpenter's glue and tape the splinter shut for an hour or so. Another option is "Super-Phatic" glue — a chemically thinned carpenter's glue sometimes available from larger hobby shops or online.

A WORD ABOUT (NON-HUMAN) POWERED TOOLS

I still use a few electrically powered tools in my shop. I'm not willing to exasperate bursitis, old rotor-cuff injuries and carpal tunnel problems to maintain the purity of hand-ripping long boards to width, hand-resawing thick stock into thin stock or hand-sawing and hand-planing large volumes of rough lumber true and to dimension. This is especially true for the times when I build larger-than-furniture-scale projects, such as reproduction gypsy caravans and small open boats that require extensive ripping of long, and often curved, parts. When I do get out components for most of my furniture projects, however, I use hand tools exclusively for ripping and planing the stock to size as well as all the joinery — the parts aren't that large and the hand tools aren't that slow. Plus I like the piece and quiet (and dust-free) nature of working with them!

Note: Even if I wanted to hand dimension my lumber, I would need a specialized frame saw for resawing, a timber saw for getting ripping planks out of cants, and a young and willing apprentice who would work the other end of these two-handled saws and would push a handplane from dusk to dawn for peanuts. Needless to say, I don't have any of these amenities in my shop! Plus I'm allergic to peanuts.

So for the times when I'm in need of resawing; of ripping long, thick boards into narrower pieces; and when I need to saw out more than a few long and narrow components, I've equipped my shop with a band saw. While mine is a larger version (it features a 17" span between the blade and the support column), a 12 or 14" saw would handle the size of stock used by most furniture makers. Because I don't use plywood in any of my projects, and because I make all my joints with hand tools, I have found no use whatsoever for a table saw in my new traditional, hand tool-primary woodworking shop.

Because I buy my lumber already surfaced (or "skip planed" to plus or minus 1/32") from the local hardwood lumber yard I have also not found much need for a thickness planer. While a power jointer is nice to have when dealing with more than a couple of long, thick pieces of lumber (I did borrow one when making my benchtops), I have found that I can, as the result of practice, easily and quickly edge plane straight and true (or true enough for most applications) typical furniture-scale components with my trusty #8 jointer plane.

In the interest of full disclosure, I do use a drill press for drilling critically accurate holes in

hardware (or for hardware) and occasionally when making holes for mortises. (I'm gravitating toward produce mortises exclusively with mortise chisels and a mallet.) I also have a small lathe for turning tool handles, making pens to give away at Christmas and for producing the occasional furniture or boat component. Finally, I maintain a stable of electric drills for the repetitive drilling of all manner of holes and for driving screw fasteners — mostly because I'm just too lazy to do these tasks with a hand drill and driver.

What I don't have in this shop are electric powered routers or sanders. I do all the things a router can by using hand tools, and I almost never make any surface smooth with sandpaper. Nearly every surface that appears in any of my projects is sheared by a plane, chisel, rasp, file or scraper. I don't miss the dust, I don't miss the noise and I don't miss the dull finish that sanding produces. More on that brag later!

Sharpening

You've probably read it hundreds of times in magazines, books and blogs and you'll read it again here: Proper sharpening is absolutely crucial to the performance, not to mention the enjoyment, of hand-powered woodworking. When you get chisels sharp (which means as sharp as they are designed to be sharpened), you can pare almost effortlessly across end grain, raising a shaving. When you get planes sharp they will also raise end grain shavings and, when set for smoothing, can plane with or against the grain without complaint. When you get saws sharp, they cut through the wood and right to a lay out

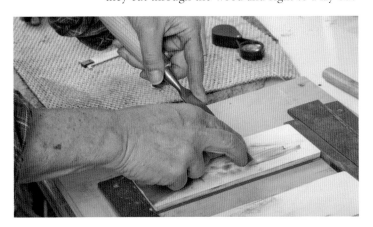

line with only a minimum amount of power or guidance from your hand. No joke!

So how do you get these tools that sharp? There are many ways of getting there but the best ways all have two attributes in common: the method is simple and ensures consistency. I have tried nearly all the typical systems, from oilstones to waterwheels and waterstones to ceramic stones to wet and dry sandpaper. After literally years of experimentation, I have finally settled on a rather eclectic system that works perfectly for the particular ways I use my tools while honoring the imperatives of simplicity and consistency.

Sharpening Station Equipment

To ensure that sharpening is always a simple and quick thing to do (which encourages you to stop and do it) it's important to have an area in the shop dedicated to this task. All the tools for sharpening should be out and ready to go; all the light you need to see what you are doing should be available with a flick of a switch; and you should never, ever place anything there — even temporarily — that would get in your way and add even ten seconds to the process.

The Sharpening Process

The following describes my basic process for sharpening chisels and plane irons. My techniques for sharpening handsaws, scrapers, drawknives, spokeshaves, molding planes and auger and center bits are standard trade practice and can be learned (as I learned them) through various books and videos (see the Resources section for sources).

ESTABLISHING PRIMARY BEVELS

I establish the primary bevel of my chisels and plane irons on a 10" waterwheel (mine is made by Tormek). Another option (which I use at my school) is a slow speed (1,725 rpm) grinder with a non-burning, aluminum oxide "cool" stone. In this case, you should go with at least an 8" wheel and be very careful, even with these stones, not to burn the edge. Precautions include constantly dipping the blade in water every few strokes; not grinding all the way to the very edge (especially important when working with A2 steel); going slow and applying just enough pressure to hold the blade in the correct position to the wheel; and lifting the blade off the stone at the end of each side sweep (rather than holding it against the wheel as you reverse direction, as doing so imparts a curve to the edge and increases the changes of overheating).

It is also possible to establish the primary bevel of plane and chisel blades using coarse sharpening stones or sandpaper adhered to a flat surface. For accuracy, I strongly suggest that you use a jig to hold the blade at the desired primary angle. Because you will be subsequently forming a micro bevel at the cutting edge, it isn't necessary to hone or polish the primary bevel. In the photo, middle right, I'm forming the bevel on a sheet of sticky-backed sandpaper (starting at 120 grit and finishing at 380) that I've adhered to a sheet of ¼" thick plate glass supported on my dead-flat bench. I'm holding the blade in the Veritas Mark II sharpening jig.

If the backs of the chisels or plane irons need flattening (and most do) I tape 400 wet and dry paper to my granite slab (a sink cutout from a counter-making shop) and lubricate it with a light oil or WD-40. If necessary, I'll start with 220-grit before going up to the 400. I finish the backs of chisels by polishing them on the waterstones up to 8,000. I don't bother polishing any of the plane irons that will receive a back bevel

Primary bevel being formed on Tormek.

Primary bevel being formed on sandpaper.

Flattening the back of a chisel on sandpaper applied to a granite slab.

(and most of the blades for bench planes do). The back bevel is only about 1° to 2° to ease sharpening — though I've gone up to 15° for raising the effective cutting angle when needed in a smoothing plane to deal with difficult grain.

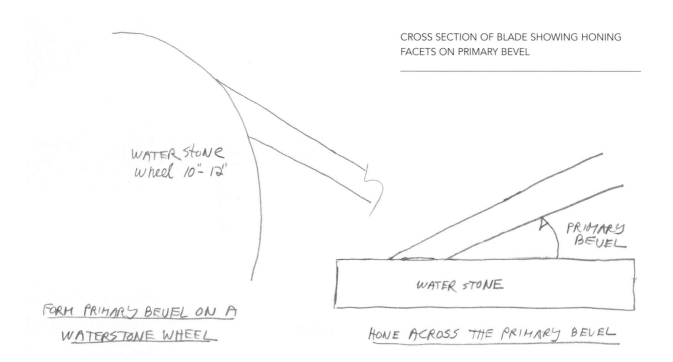

WATER STONE
wheel 10"-12"

PRIMARY
BEVEL

WATER STONE

FORM PRIMARY BEVEL ON A
WATERSTONE WHEEL

HONE ACROSS THE PRIMARY BEVEL

HONING STRAIGHT-EDGED BLADES

Honing across a slightly hollow primary bevel
is my method of choice for sharpening chisels
and for plane blades that have a straight edge and
are used bevel-side up. This includes most block
plane and joinery plane blades (such as rabbet,
plow and edging). This sharpening method does
not raise the cutting angle of the blade as does
the microbevel method — this is a real benefit
when planing or paring across end grain where

Closeup of hands holding a plane blade on stone, primary
bevel flat to stone.

the lower the angle, the smoother and easier the
cut. Note that you do have to use a wheel to
form the primary bevel for this method to work.

The hollow bevel method is also the most consistent and easiest method for freehand sharpening:
You simply hold the primary bevel down on the
stone — easy to do because it's so wide — and

Stones being lapped on a lapping plate. One pencil-crosshatched stone is shown.

draw the blade back toward you six to eight times. I start on a 1,000 grit waterstone, and then move up to a 4,000 or 8,000 stone for polishing and for removing the burr on the flat back. If I know I'm going to be dealing with some tricky grain, I'll go to my 16,000 ceramic stone for stropping. (You can substitute a flat piece of hardwood imbued with buffing compound for this pricey stone.)

Be sure, though, that you are starting with flat stones — I flatten mine regularly on a diamond-infused lapping plate. A strip of 120 to 180 grit sandpaper adhered to a flat piece of glass or granite works well also. To see where I'm at during the flattening process, I first crosshatch the surface of the stone with a pencil. I then rub the stone on the lapping plate in small circular movements. When the crosshatch is completely erased, the stone is flat and ready to transfer this newly flattened reference surface to the bevel and to the back of the cutting blade, ensuring the sharpest edge possible.

When sharpening a plane blade, I usually lift up the back slightly with a thin metal rule placed along one edge of the stone to create about a 1°

Using a ruler in creating a low-angle back bevel.

back bevel. This polishes the back of the blade right where it meets the tip creating a super-sharp edge. I have yet to encounter any reason not to do this step, and it ensures the sharpest edge possible in the minimum amount of time. Be aware, however, that you cannot employ this trick on chisels as the back of a chisel is sometimes used as a reference surface when held flat to the board or to a guide block.

Setting blade to shop-made jig.

Setting blade to Veritas jig.

HONING PLANE BLADES WITH A CAMBERED EDGE

When the blades are cambered — as are most of my bench plane blades except for block and rabbet plane blades — I find it difficult to freehand a microbevel with a high level of consistency. Instead, I fix the blade into a jig and hone a microbevel at a 3°- to 5°- steeper angle than the primary bevel. When I use my narrow-wheeled guide (made by Eclipse) I set the angle by holding the blade to a stop fixed to a piece of wood. When using the Veritas Mark II jig, I use the jig's removable guide to set the angle. With either jig, I find that I can better concentrate on keeping pressure right where the blade touches the stone by pushing, rather than pulling the jig (see pictures below). To make an even microbevel across the width of the cambered blade, I start on the 1,000 grit stone (which I've checked and lapped flat if necessary) and focus the pressure for seven or eight strokes on one side of the blade, then an equal amount on the opposite far side. I then make five or six strokes just to either side of the middle, then finish with a few strokes right in the center. I repeat the process with a few less strokes on my 8,000 polishing stone, then use the ruler trick to make a back bevel and to take the burr off the back of the blade on the same stone.

Pushing against the blade (away from user) set in an eclipse jig.

The same view with a Veritas jig.

HONING BACK BEVELS

When sharpening a standard, bevel-down blade (for smoothing difficult grain without causing tear-out), you will want to hone a significant back bevel on the flat back of the blade. This step turns your standard, 45° plane into a high-angle smoothing plane. To do the back bevel, set up the sharpened blade bevel-side-up in your sharpening jig and index it to make a bevel of 10° to 15°. The back bevel changes the effective cutting angle of your standard plane from 45° to 55° or 60°. At this angle, the fibers separate quickly and cleanly from the wood's surface. The downsides are first: the plane will be harder to push (higher back pressure) and second, the blade will tend to dull faster (more work=more heat=accelerated degradation of the cutting edge).

SHARPENING GOUGES, AND HOLLOW AND ROUND PLANE BLADES

I have found that a 1"-wide motorized belt sander set up with specialized abrasive belts followed by a leather belt infused with rubbing compound to be a fast and safe way to create, and then hone, the curved bevels of gouges and rounded-edge plane blades (as found in scrub planes and molding planes). Though you still need to be careful about burning the edge (i.e. ruining the temper) the low speed of the belt coupled with careful monitoring for discoloration avoids that problem. To remove the burr on the inside of the gouge, I pull the blade back along a curved slipstone or a dowel to which I've glued 1,000 grit wet and dry sandpaper.

To hone a microbevel on the inside curve of a hollow plane blade I use either cylindrical waterstones (1,000 followed by 8,000) or a dowel to which I've affixed wet and dry sandpaper (400 followed by 1,000). I remove the burr by rolling and pulling the back of the blade on a flat stone.

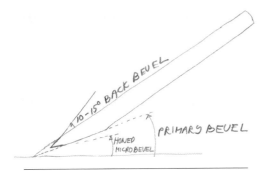

CONFIGURATION OF BACK BEVEL IN
A SMOOTHING PLANE

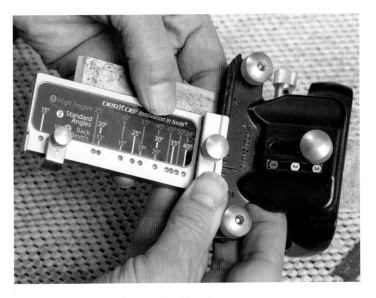

Closeup of a Veritas jig showing a back bevel setup.

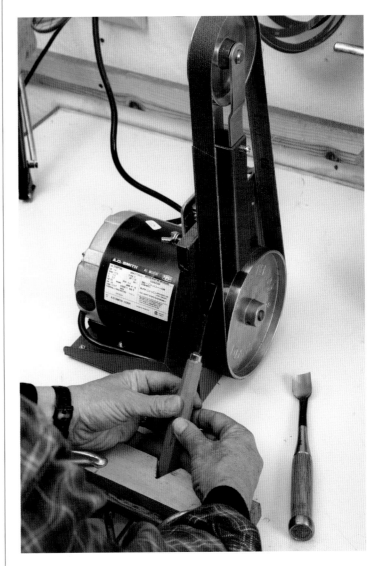

A vertical 1"-wide belt sander.

SECTION TWO

SHOP PROJECTS

Now let's get you working in your new shop and, taking the tools in hand, create the layout tools, fixtures and furnishings you need for working wood in the most efficient and enjoyable way possible. In the making of these essential accessories you will learn to choose the appropriate tools and practice the essential skills that enable hand-powered tools to work the way they were intended. Please note that you'll do so at a lower risk than if you were trying out these new skills on projects that will leave the shop! The projects here are ordered to present progressively more challenging techniques and tools while allowing you to practice previously introduced skills. In most cases, you will actually use the accessory you just made to help build the next one.

Of course, the most fundamental shop tool you need for working wood with hand tools is a workbench. However, because the building of a workbench is a decidedly advanced project (due to its large scale and its construction from dense hardwoods), we are going to assume that you have one. Refer back to the discussion of workbenches in Section 1, on page 21 to learn how to select a bench. It's worth repeating here that no matter what type of bench you choose, it should meet three fundamental criteria. First: The top should be flat (if it isn't, you can flatten it with handplanes following the same process shown on page 169 for flattening a board). Second: The bench should be sturdy enough to not shake when you plane or saw a board on it. Third: It should be the right height for you to bear down on a handplane, yet tall enough to see what you are doing when sawing or paring to a cutline. (You will likely have to find a compromise height between the two; or build a fixture that raises the bench for precision sawing and paring work; or do as I did and install a second, dedicated-task bench.)

The Projects

The first three projects that you'll build are exceedingly simple, yet essential tools for doing layouts and for checking the "truth" of a board: a straightedge (shown above), a try square and a pair of winding sticks (below). You'll use the straightedge to check a board's surface for flatness and its edge for straightness. The try square lays out 90° angles (ubiquitous in furnituremaking), while the winding sticks tell you at a glance if (and how much and in what direction) the board is twisted.

The bench fixtures that you'll build go a long way toward keeping life simple and pleasurable for working wood by hand. The two planing stops, one for edges and one for faces, allow you to deal with shorter, narrow boards (which generally means most of the components of a furniture piece) without having to constantly take the time to open a vise, hold the board level, set a bench stop if necessary for additional support, and then close the vise down. A pair of bench hooks instantly provide support for stock that you need to hold to make crosscuts for joints or to cut to length. This stop can also serve as a shooting board to hold a board in perfect alignment with a plane running on its edge so that you can, in just a few strokes, true a rough end crosscut accurately to within a thousandth of an inch. The sticking board holds narrow workpieces up off the bench so you can use a plow plane to cut grooves and to support stock securely for shaping with molding planes. Finally, you'll build a small tote featuring a floating bottom panel; lapped corner joints; and a divider/carry handle set into a stopped dado. On my bench, this tote keeps small layout tools, scraps of leather and blocks of wood organized and close at hand.

Edge planing stop in use.

Face planing stop in use.

Face planing stop in use with thicker board – tilted up in vise.

Bench hooks in use.

Sticking board in use.

Bench tote filled with items, handy and ready to go to work.

To ensure that you get the most you can out of building these tools and fixtures, I will give you the following information for each project:

- **The Project**: A full understanding of what the tool or bench accessory does, why you need it and how you use it.
- **The Skillset:** The skills and procedures you'll learn in building it.
- **The Toolset:** The tools you'll learn to use.
- **The Process:** A step-by-step guide to building the project that includes how to select the wood and how to choose and use the tools (including appropriate bench fixtures and tool accessories) in the most efficient way.

Working Wood by Hand: The Mindset

Pre-industrial artisans worked wood with the same goal aspired to by modern industrial tradesman: To turn out a product as quickly as possible in order to make a profit. Though as New Traditional Woodworkers, profit isn't our goal or motivation, understanding and learning to use hand tools in the most efficient way is. Efficiency makes the work go as easily, and therefore as enjoyably, as possible. To achieve a high level of efficiency, however, it's not just a matter of rote learning to use the tools correctly — it's also important to understand why it's the correct way to use them. The following fundamental concepts underlay all the techniques you will be learning as you build the projects presented in the remainder of the book:

TOOLS MUST BE TUNED AND SHARP
Because it is your body that is providing the energy source for the tools (all $\frac{1}{15}$th horsepower of it!), the ability to sharpen and properly set up or configure a tool becomes paramount to not only efficiency but accuracy for this fundamental reason: The less effort you need to power a hand tool through the wood, the more control you gain over its force and direction.

'TIS A GIFT TO BE SIMPLE (AND TO PRACTICE AT IT)
The underlying goal of hand processing is to find the simplest way to perform a specific task — because the simplest way is invariably the most efficient way, as it requires the least amount of energy, the fewest number of strokes and the fewest number of tools. Once you discover (or are shown) the simplest way, you practice the method to refine it and to get faster at it. As your accuracy at sawing to a line increases, for example, the number of time-consuming paring strokes with a chisel to clean up the cut goes down … eventually you'll be making tight-fitting joints right off the saw that require no chisel work at all.

FROM COARSE TO FINE
A fundamental way to speed up hand tool work is to use coarse — and therefore fast — waste-removal tools such as hatchets, drawknives and scrub planes to bring stock close to size prior to shaping with slower-acting (and more time-consuming to sharpen) tools such as spokeshaves and standard bench planes.

GOOD ENOUGH IS GOOD ENOUGH
To further the goal of efficiency, you must determine where formed joints are needed and where you can get away with simple mechanical fastening. For example, you might choose pocket screws to hold a top board down to the case side framing instead of fashioning through, wedged mortise and tenons. If you do go with a formed joint, you don't need to go overboard. As a general rule, joints don't need to be overly large or deep. For example, tenons (and their time-consuming to make mortises) don't have to be deeper than 1" or so to be strong in furniture work as additional strength comes via the shoulder connection. As another example, dadoes and rabbets don't have to be that deep to be strong because the compressive strength of wood against its end grain is enormous.

MAXIMIZE THE MINIMIZATION OF MISTAKES
Because mistakes can be significantly time consuming in hand tool work, they must be avoided. Make clear reference marks not just for cutlines, but to indicate waste (the part being cut away) and to keep the parts oriented correctly. The traditional layout methods that I show here minimize mistakes through the use of dividers, gauges, templates and tick sticks. Machine tool methods of calculating, reading and marking from numerical cutlists and rulers (required because the machines need numbers for calibration) aren't really necessary for hand tool woodworking.

The Cabinetmaker's Shop, Elias Pozelius, from *Orbus Pictus nach Zeichnugen der Susanna Maria Sandrart — Nurnberg*, 1690.

GEOMETRY TRUMPS ARITHMETIC

Before the Industrial Revolution and the mechanization of the woodworking process, the design and layout of furniture (and its forbearer, architecture) in the Western world was largely based on the "classic orders" of proportion and geometry. Instead of working to measurements, artisans started with a fixed parameter (i.e. a traditional pattern, the width of a board, a fixed dimension for height or width, an object that had to be enclosed, etc.) and then applied whole-number proportions to create the overall dimensions of the piece. From there, every element of the piece was derived from simple geometric forms that were proportioned in whole-number ratios and laid out with dividers, squares and straightedges. Because every element had some proportional or intersectional relationship with each other, the result was a fundamentally simple and pleasing design.

FITTING PIECE-TO-PIECE

In machine-process furnituremaking, most of the components are precut to size (to a numerical cutlist to which the machine's indexing system is set) and then are fitted together during final assembly. In hand tool woodworking, efficiency is better achieved through the opposite approach: you lay out the first part (usually to a tick stick, divider or a template); cut and pare to the cutlines; then directly size the next component to fit to this first one. The entire project is built piece-by-piece, sizing one component to the next; transferring the location of the component directly to its mating surface; and transcribing the male elements of a joint directly to define the female. This approach makes layouts go quickly, while at the same time reducing to nearly zero any chance of errors in the layout, the fitting of pieces and the mating of joints.

GETTING A GRIP

When working wood by hand, you bring the tools to the wood — but when machining wood you usually bring the wood to the tools. In either case, however, you need to somehow ensure a firm connection between the wood and the tool's reference surfaces. For machine tools, this means you (or a power feeder or a pneumatic clamp system!) hold the wood to the machine's fences and stop systems. For us hand tool folks, it's the opposite: We have to secure the wood firmly and then move the hand tool along the board while holding the tool's reference surface (such as the sole of a bench plane or the fence of a joinery plane) tightly against it.

Even if we had three hands, however, it wouldn't be enough. For safety sake as well as for the sake of efficiency, we need ways to hold the wood securely against slipping and even vibration. This task should almost never involve one of our hands. Instead, this is what the vises, iron holddfasts, shop-made fixtures and temporary wedges and other clamping devices installed on our solid workbenches are for! The goal in working wood with hand tools is that the only thing moving should be the tool and never the wood.

TOOL SLAVING

The most efficient sizing of certain joints (the mortise and tenon is a prime example) is often a result of "tool slaving." This process involves gauging the width of a joint to the width of the tool that will be used to remove the waste material. For example, to make a mortise with a single chisel you would size a mortise to the width of one of your mortise chisels. This enables you to chop out the length of the mortise in a single run, avoiding having to step the chisel over to take a second run in order to widen the mortise — a step that would slow you down and reduce your chances of making an accurate joint. Likewise, you would size the width of a dado to a certain paring chisel. Tool slaving might not sound like a big deal until you consider how many mortises, dados and other tool-slaved joints might be required in a typical piece of furniture.

TOOL TRACKING

When building rectilinear objects such as traditional furniture — which are essentially planer surfaces that relate to one another at certain, fixed angles — the building process is all about creating and then working from true (i.e. flat and straight) reference surfaces. When you use a tool to plane, chisel or saw the board, you register one of the tool's inherent reference surfaces (such as the sole of a bench plane, the fence of a joinery plane, the back of a chisel or the blade of a saw) to a true reference surface: either to a trued face or edge, or to a trued layout line. Assuming you handle the tool properly, you'll transmit the tool's true surface to the workpiece via the tool's cutter. With practice you can also take advantage of the tendency of hand tools to self-register to their own "tool tracks," or to ones that you establish for them.

To make this rather complex concept clear, let's run through a few examples.

To begin the truing process on a board, you start with the primary reference surface in your shop: the trued surface of your workbench. With the first piece of wood cut to a component's approximate dimensions, you register its face to the trued benchtop. If it isn't true to the bench (i.e. it rocks or shows gaps), you change the board's face with a plane until it registers true to the benchtop.

To create a true edge along the side of the board, you lay out a straight line on the face from a known straightedge (that's the first tool we'll make in this book) then plane to this line. A handplane will create a surface as true to straight as its sole is straight. To make the edge perpendicular to the trued face of the board, you check with a try square, holding its body to the reference face and adjusting the edge's angle with the plane until the square's blade says the edge is true.

To saw the end of the board true, you draw a layout line by registering the leg of the square to the trued reference edge, scribing a line to create a track for the sawblade and then you saw off the waste. Once the teeth are engaged in the wood, the blade of the saw self-registers to the walls of its own kerf (its tool track), helping you maintain a straight and accurate cut throughout the cut. To bring the accuracy of the end cut to within a thousandth of an inch, you would "shoot" the end of the board with a plane laid on its side.

As a final example, when you need to chisel to a reference line (that might, for example, delineate the base of a lap joint), you would scribe a knife line referenced to the square's tongue. First you would make a pin prick at the location of the joint's shoulder (probably established with the point of a divider or by using a marking knife set to a location on a tick stick). You would then hold the tip of your marking knife in the pin hole, slide the blade of the square over to bear against it, and then scribe the line along the blade. You might deepen the scribe line by knifing a bevel cut into it from the waste side of the line to create a little "wall." The result is a tool track that precisely and securely registers the flat back of the chisel for chopping the shoulder of the joint.

"Handtool-friendly" Wood

When you work wood with hand tools — which means working with that meager $\frac{1}{15}$th horsepower — you really do need all the help you can get! You quickly discover the importance of choosing the right tool for a particular task; of tuning and sharpening its cutter to its maximum potential; of handling and orienting the tool properly; and, finally, of using your muscles (and gravity whenever possible) in the most efficient way. There is, however, an easy way to get help: you can choose wood that is "handtool friendly."

Wood friendly to hand tools is soft enough to work easily (i.e. you can shear its fibers with a plane relatively easily) yet not so soft that it tends to "mush" under the pressure of a smooth plane or when you pare across its grain with a chisel. It also must not be so soft that it crushes or deforms at joints when stressed (which often creates permanent gaps) or that light impacts from harder objects easily dent it. Either of these weaknesses would make the wood a poor choice for use

HANDTOOL-FRIENDLY AMERICAN FURNITURE WOODS

Comments	Common Furniture Wood Species	Specific Gravity (@12% m.c.)	Stability		Strength and Hardness	
Colonial and Shaker	Pine	.36				
Good for carving	Basswood	.37				
"Poorman's Cherry" good training wood	Alder	.41				
Ugly + spongy	Poplar	.42	More stable		Easier working	
Ideal for hand-tool produced furniture of all styles	Ash	.49				
	Cherry	.50		Less stable		Harder to work
	Western Maple and Red	.54				
	Walnut	.55				
Used for components and projects where strength is a priority	Eastern "Hard" Maple	.63				
	Red Oak	.63				
	White Oak	.68				
	Hickory	.72				

Notes: A) Density can vary within species and even within a specific tree — so characteristics may vary from this chart.

B) In general, the higher the wood's specific gravity, the denser the wood and, as a result, the more tendency for the wood to change dimension as its internal moisture content varies.

C) In general, denser woods are tougher on cutting edges and require more force to work than less dense woods.

in furniture. Friendly wood must also drill easily, but not so easily that its fibers strip out around the screw threads when placed under a modest amount of tension. Finally, if you're going to put all that effort into making something by hand, you're going to want that wood to be stable (not shrink or expand too much) and to be beautiful in hue and texture.

Fortunately for us, beautiful, hand tool-friendly wood is indigenous to North America. It is relatively inexpensive and easy to find through local sawyers in some areas of the country and at hardwood lumberyards often located in the larger metropolitan areas. While you may be tempted by the rich beauty of tropical imports such as sapele and bubinga that will beckon to you at the specialty yards, you would soon discover that working them by hand is a challenge. Their dense, cross-grained fibers push back hard and easily tear out, demanding both the sharpest of tools and high physical exertion to push your tools smoothly through the wood. Of course, not all tropical hardwoods are that demanding — but those that aren't (such as Honduras mahogany — the wood of choice of early American cabinetmakers) are rare and quite expensive.

Let's take a closer look at our domestic woods: Though some are a bit too hard and others are too soft, a great many are perfect for hand tool woodworking as you can see in the chart below. Fortuitously, some of the best hand tool-friendly woods are also the most beautiful. When I teach hand tool woodworking, I nearly always start people out with our local northwest red alder. In my experience this wood is one of the friendliest of all the commonly available, kiln-dried domestic species. It planes and pares easily and leaves a smooth surface without being too soft; it's strong enough for small furniture projects; and while not as beautifully grained as cherry (which it's closest to in hue), it is still quite attractive. Cherry, red maple and walnut, falling in the middle of the chart have been, and continue to be, North America's premium furniture woods and are a pleasure to work by hand.

Boards stacked for acclimation.

Acclimating the Wood

Whether you buy your furniture wood from a specialty hardwood lumberyard or from a local sawyer, the chance that the wood is ready to go into a piece of furniture with a minimum risk of shrinking (or, rarely, expanding) unduly is just about nil. Instead, it's more likely (at least in most areas of the United States) that the wood has been sitting in an unheated space and is, at best, in equilibrium with the ambient moisture content of the outside environment — even if the wood has been kiln dried. That's not good. You want the wood in your furniture piece to be in equilibrium with your area's typical home environment.

Luckily, it's not that hard to get it that way — it just takes a little time and forethought. In my neck of the woods, the hardwood lumber at the dealers sits in an unheated warehouse where humidity generally reaches about 11 percent to 12 percent as measured by an electric moisture meter. I need to get the wood to around 8 percent to 9 percent,

Moisture meters, pin style at left, and pinless (non-marring) above.

MOISTURE CONTENT EQUILIBRIUM CHART
(FROM THE U.S. FOREST PRODUCTS LAB)

Temperature (dry-bulb)	Relative Humidity																			
	5	10	15	20	25	30	35	40	45	50	55	60	65	70	75	80	85	90	95	98
°F	Percent																			
30	1.4	2.6	3.7	4.6	5.5	6.3	7.1	7.9	8.7	9.5	10.4	11.3	12.4	13.5	14.9	16.5	18.5	21.0	24.3	26.9
40	1.4	2.6	3.7	4.6	5.5	6.3	7.1	7.9	8.7	9.5	10.4	11.3	12.3	13.5	14.9	16.5	18.5	21.0	24.3	26.9
50	1.4	2.6	3.6	4.6	5.5	6.3	7.1	7.9	8.7	9.5	10.3	11.2	12.3	13.4	14.8	16.4	18.4	20.9	24.3	26.9
60	1.3	2.5	3.6	4.6	5.4	6.2	7.0	7.8	8.6	9.4	10.2	11.1	12.1	13.3	14.6	16.2	18.2	20.7	24.1	26.8
70	1.3	2.5	3.5	4.5	5.4	6.2	6.9	7.7	8.5	9.2	10.1	11.0	12.0	13.1	14.4	16.0	17.9	20.5	23.9	26.6
80	1.3	2.4	3.5	4.4	5.3	6.1	6.8	7.6	8.3	9.1	9.9	10.8	11.7	12.9	14.2	15.7	17.7	20.2	23.6	26.3
90	1.2	2.3	3.4	4.3	5.1	5.9	6.7	7.4	8.1	8.9	9.7	10.5	11.5	12.6	13.9	15.4	17.3	19.8	23.3	26.0
100	1.2	2.3	3.3	4.2	5.0	5.8	6.5	7.2	7.9	8.7	9.5	10.3	11.2	12.3	13.6	15.1	17.0	19.5	23.9	25.6
110	1.1	2.2	3.2	4.0	4.9	5.6	6.3	7.0	7.7	8.4	9.2	10.0	11.0	12.0	13.2	14.7	16.6	19.1	22.4	25.2
120	1.1	2.1	3.0	3.9	4.7	5.4	6.1	6.8	7.5	8.2	8.9	9.7	10.6	11.7	12.9	14.4	16.2	18.6	22.0	24.7
130	1.0	2.0	2.9	3.7	4.5	5.2	5.9	6.6	7.2	7.9	8.7	9.4	10.3	11.3	12.5	14.0	15.8	18.2	21.5	24.2
140	.9	1.9	2.8	3.6	4.3	5.0	5.7	6.3	7.0	7.7	8.4	9.1	10.0	11.0	12.1	13.6	15.3	17.7	21.0	23.7
150	.9	1.8	2.6	3.4	4.1	4.8	5.5	6.1	6.7	7.4	8.1	8.8	9.7	10.6	11.8	13.1	14.9	17.2	20.4	23.1
160	.8	1.6	2.4	3.2	3.9	4.6	5.2	5.8	6.4	7.1	7.8	8.5	9.3	10.3	11.4	12.7	14.4	16.7	19.9	22.5
170	.7	1.5	2.3	3.0	3.7	4.3	4.9	5.6	6.2	6.8	7.4	8.2	9.0	9.9	11.0	12.3	14.0	16.2	19.3	21.9
180	.7	1.4	2.1	2.8	3.5	4.1	4.7	5.3	5.9	6.5	7.1	7.8	8.6	9.5	10.5	11.8	13.5	15.7	18.7	21.3
190	.6	1.3	1.9	2.6	3.2	3.8	4.4	5.0	5.5	6.1	6.8	7.5	8.2	9.1	10.1	11.4	13.0	15.1	18.1	20.7
200	.5	1.1	1.7	2.4	3.0	3.5	4.1	4.6	5.2	5.8	6.4	7.1	7.8	8.7	9.7	10.9	12.5	14.6	17.5	20.0
210	.5	1.0	1.6	2.1	2.7	3.2	3.8	4.3	4.9	5.4	6.0	6.7	7.4	8.3	9.2	10.4	12.0	14.0	16.9	19.3
220	.4	.9	1.4	1.9	2.4	2.9	3.4	3.9	4.5	5.0	5.6	6.3	7.0	7.8	8.8	9.9	*	*	*	*
230	.3	.8	1.2	1.6	2.1	2.6	3.1	3.6	4.2	4.7	5.3	6.0	6.7	*	*	*	*	*	*	*
240	.3	.6	.9	1.3	1.7	2.1	2.6	3.1	3.5	4.1	4.6	*	*	*	*	*	*	*	*	*
250	.2	.4	.7	1.0	1.3	1.7	2.1	2.5	2.9	*	*	*	*	*	*	*	*	*	*	*
260	.2	.3	.5	.7	.9	1.1	1.4	*	*	*	*	*	*	*	*	*	*	*	*	*
270	.1	.1	.2	.3	.4	.4	*	*	*	*	*	*	*	*	*	*	*	*	*	*

¹Asterisks indicate conditions not possible at atmospheric pressure.

Some Examples: In New England and in the Northwest, the average home temperatures hover around 70° while the ambient humidity is about 45 percent percent. The table indicates that the moisture content level of furniture-ready wood should be at 8.5 percent percent to be in equilibrium with this environment. In the much drier Southwest, the average moisture content level would be around 6 percent percent. In the wetter Southeast, you are looking at around 11 percent percent.

(the point at which it will be in equilibrium with our regional home's environment of around 70° and an ambient humidity of 45 percent — according to the chart produced by the U.S. Forest Products Lab as shown in chart above). To accomplish this, I have gotten into the habit of purchasing the wood at least two to three weeks ahead of time. I carefully stack the wood on a flat surface in my shop with stickers set in between each board to allow the air to circulate and the wood to "breathe" (see top picture on page 77).

Because my shop is in my house (one of the joys of a hand tool-primary woodworking shop), I can get away with stacking it here because the shop enjoys the same environment the furniture will live in. If your shop is damp and/or marginally heated, you will want to stack the wood inside your house somewhere until you are ready to work with it. If your project is going to have to endure periods of inactivity, get in the habit of bringing the work pieces back into the house between work sessions.

Selecting Wood for Stability

Assuming your wood has reached moisture content equilibrium with the environment in which it's going to live out its life as a piece of furniture, let's consider what else might affect its stability. We would like to know how resistant the wood is to shrinkage and expansion and, perhaps more importantly, to twisting. (The latter can permanently rack a piece of furniture.) To make a prediction about the wood you are about to use, study the boards for the following factors:

SPECIES-SPECIFIC ISSUES
As a general rule, the denser the wood, the more potential it has for changing dimension (width and thickness only — wood doesn't change significantly along its length) relative to changes in ambient conditions.

ENVIRONMENTAL-SPECIFIC ISSUES
An individual tree's exposure to strong prevailing winds, to poor soil, and/or to high altitude (among other factors) are stresses that can skew the typical stability and workability characteristics of the species. You have to look at the lumber to check for stress indicators such as twisted grain along its length (which will invariably cause warping); or for ripple-graining (when fibers quickly switch grain direction they are difficult to plane smoothly); or for inclusions of pitch, bark or even rocks (which are a cutting edge's ultimate nightmare)!

TREE-INDIVIDUAL-SPECIFIC ISSUES
From what portion of the tree the lumber was taken can also affect the stability of the wood. Your boards will hopefully have come from near the base of the tree. If the tree was of a good size, the wood taken from here tends to be stiff, stable and free of knots. The further away the boards are taken from the base, the more chance the wood has grown near branches and has been stressed (because the wood is compressed under a branch). It will also likely exhibit grain runoff along the edges or display knots on the faces (or echoes of knots) because of its proximity to the off-shooting branches. Knots quickly dull chisels and hand-planes, and grain runoff can weaken the board and/or cause it to bow along its length over time.

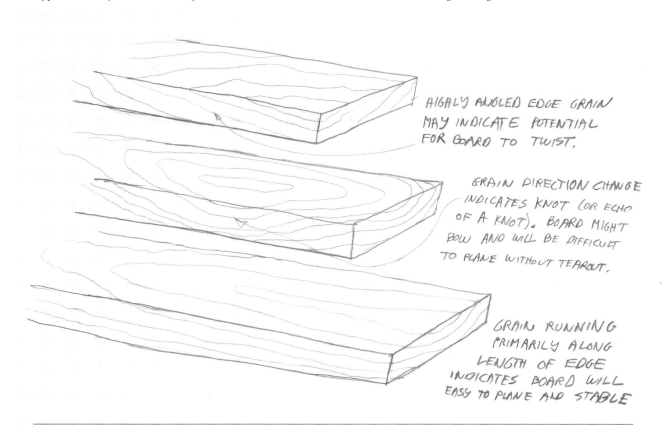

HIGHLY ANGLED EDGE GRAIN MAY INDICATE POTENTIAL FOR BOARD TO TWIST.

GRAIN DIRECTION CHANGE INDICATES KNOT (OR ECHO OF A KNOT). BOARD MIGHT BOW AND WILL BE DIFFICULT TO PLANE WITHOUT TEAROUT.

GRAIN RUNNING PRIMARILY ALONG LENGTH OF EDGE INDICATES BOARD WILL EASY TO PLANE AND STABLE

BOARD CONDITIONS INDICATED BY EDGE GRAIN

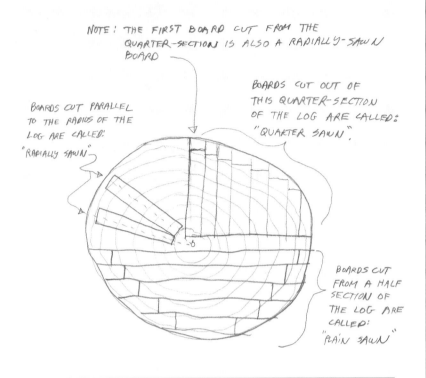

NOTE: THE FIRST BOARD CUT FROM THE QUARTER-SECTION IS ALSO A RADIALLY-SAWN BOARD

BOARDS CUT PARALLEL TO THE RADIUS OF THE LOG ARE CALLED: "RADIALLY SAWN"

BOARDS CUT OUT OF THIS QUARTER-SECTION OF THE LOG ARE CALLED: "QUARTER SAWN"

BOARDS CUT FROM A HALF SECTION OF THE LOG ARE CALLED: "PLAIN SAWN"

CROSS SECTION OF TREE WITH BOARD ORIENTATIONS LABELED

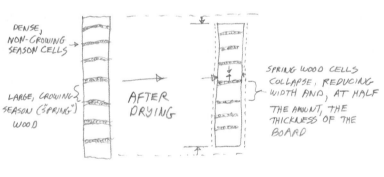

DENSE, NON-GROWING SEASON CELLS

LARGE, GROWING SEASON ("SPRING") WOOD

AFTER DRYING

SPRING WOOD CELLS COLLAPSE, REDUCING WIDTH AND, AT HALF THE AMOUNT, THE THICKNESS OF THE BOARD

RADIAL SAWN

PLAIN SAWN

SPRING WOOD CELLS COLLAPSE, PULLING FACES OF THE BOARD INTO A CUP.

HOW AND WHY PLAIN-SAWN BOARDS CUP; QUARTERSAWN DON'T

MILLING-SPECIFIC ISSUES

Finally, and perhaps most importantly, you need to determine how the board is oriented relative to the center of the tree. A quick check of the end grain tells you whether it was cut parallel to the radius of the tree or tangential. If you are looking for interesting figure on a panel or tabletop, you will likely choose the latter as radially sawn (and most quartersawn) boards only reveal straight grain lines on their faces. The downside, however, is that tangentially sawn boards tend to cup as they dry as illustrated in the bottom, left drawing.

WHERE'S THE PLYWOOD IN THIS BOOK?

There isn't any because I simply can't recommend using plywood in a hand tool-primary shop. The first reason is that traditional hand tools aren't designed to work plywood (the brittle glue layers quickly dull most hand-powered steel tools), and even if they could, the energy demanded from you to cut through plywood any thicker than ¼" is very high indeed. Second, when you cut or sand plywood you create toxic dust and fumes. Some people (including a number of retired cabinetmakers I know personally) are highly allergic to these production byproducts. Finally, we don't need plywood to build any of the shop fixtures and accessories presented in this book (just as you don't need plywood to build furniture for that matter!). We just need to select the wood carefully and assemble it properly. (Plywood in the construction of casework such as kitchen cabinets and entertainment centers is another matter — and another book!)

Straightedge

Yes you really can make a highly precise (not to mention beautiful), straightedge out of a length of wood. In many ways, you'll find wood to be a better material than metal for this purpose: The wooden straightedge is lighter and easier to shift around than a metal one when testing a board; it won't ding the board if you drop it on it; and, best of all, you can quickly and easily retrue a wooden straightedge to within a half-a-thousandth of an inch with a handplane.

SKILLS INTRODUCED:

In this project you will learn how to select the wood for stability; acclimate the stock; lay out and saw a board to width and length; plane a smooth surface; lay out, shape, smooth and bevel a curved edge; plane a straight and true edge; drill a hole with a brace and bit; and apply an oil finish. Not bad for just making a stick!

TOOLS INTRODUCED:

These are the tools you will use in this project: Marking gauge; layout square; rip and crosscut handsaws; try plane; smooth plane; drawknife; rasp; file; low-angle spokeshave (or block plane); brace and bit, rubber sanding block.

THE PROCESS:

1. Select the Wood

Choose a board free of bow or twist and with straight grain running lengthwise along the edge of the board. Reject a board in which more than 20 percent of the grain lines don't make it over the run from which you'll make the straightedge). You can sometimes purchase ½"-thick stock at your hardwood lumberyard or from a local cabinetshop, or you can plane a ¾" piece to size. If that's the case, be sure to remove an equal amount of material from each face to minimize differences of moisture content. Another option, is to resaw a 4/4 board (usually $^{13}/_{16}$" thick) in half using a band saw.

The wood should be well seasoned as revealed by a moisture meter and the table of moisture content equilibrium (see chart on page 78). Less dense species such as cherry or walnut are a good choice as they are less likely to change shape with changes in ambient moisture levels. Avoid using softer wood as the reference edge may be too easily dinged. Avoid any splits or localized changes in grain direction (which are echoes of knots further away in the tree and can cause the board to warp or bow over time).

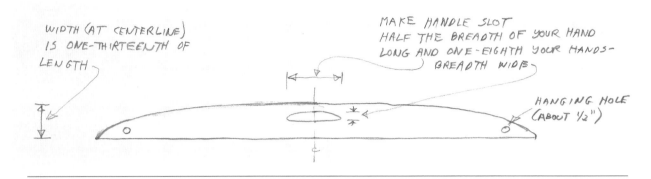

WIDTH (AT CENTERLINE) IS ONE-THIRTEENTH OF LENGTH

MAKE HANDLE SLOT HALF THE BREADTH OF YOUR HAND LONG AND ONE-EIGHTH YOUR HANDS-BREADTH WIDE

HANGING HOLE (ABOUT ½")

STRAIGHTEDGE FACE VIEW

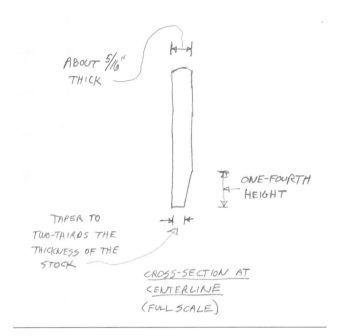

ABOUT 5/16" THICK

ONE-FOURTH HEIGHT

TAPER TO TWO-THIRDS THE THICKNESS OF THE STOCK

CROSS-SECTION AT CENTERLINE (FULL SCALE)

STRAIGHTEDGE END VIEW

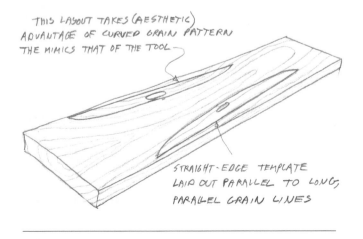

THIS LAYOUT TAKES (AESTHETIC) ADVANTAGE OF CURVED GRAIN PATTERN THE MIMICS THAT OF THE TOOL.

STRAIGHT-EDGE TEMPLATE LAID OUT PARALLEL TO LONG, PARALLEL GRAIN LINES

LAYOUT OF STRAIGHTEDGE ON BOARD TO PARALLEL GRAIN

2. Rip and Crosscut the Board to Rough Dimension

In this step you will crosscut the piece to length and then rip out a strip about ¼" wider than your finished dimension. (You almost always work in this order, because you never want to rip any more wood than you have to!) You'll make the straightedge as long as the typical length of a furniture component — about 3'. You will likely want to make another longer one for laying out and checking larger components. The width of the straightedge is ⅓th of its length (meaning a 39"-long straightedge will be 3" wide).

To make these cuts efficiently, be sure your saws are sharp and lubricated with paste wax or vegetable oil, and place the stock on a low sawbench (just under knee-cap height — 20" high works for me). This low bench height allows you to make full-length strokes with a standard-sized handsaw. You'll discover, if you haven't already, that typical contractor's sawhorses are much too high for handsaws — their height significantly shortens the length of your stroke and doesn't allow gravity to help you push the saw. You can cut down an existing set of horses, or build a pair of specialized handsaw benches as I did; the drawings for these are on page 164.

Use an 8 to 10 tpi crosscut handsaw to cut the board to rough length. You will cut it to the finished length after ripping out the strip. Lay out the cutline across the board and perpendicular across the far edge using a carpenter's square. Start the cut by making very short push strokes alongside the cutline, with your thumb knuckle guiding the blade. To prevent jamming, lift the blade just enough to take the weight of the saw off the teeth and position the blade at a low angle to the wood. The idea is to make a starting kerf long and deep enough to bury at least four teeth in the kerf before raising the blade and increasing the stroke — this prevents an individual tooth from jamming on the corner of the board when you start pushing the saw vigorously with long strokes. When you do start increasing your motion to full strokes, move your thumb at least a handbreadth away from the blade. At first, you may need to hold a square next to the saw to ensure you are making a perpendicular cut, but with practice you won't need to do this. Continue across the board holding the saw at a 45° angle to the face of the board. If your kerf starts to wander away from the cutline, don't twist the blade! Instead, lower the blade alongside the line where you want the cut to go, establishing a new kerf (a tool track) for the blade to run in. This technique also works when ripping.

With the board cut to rough length, it's time to rip it to width. Look carefully at the run of the grain of the board and try to "capture" as straight a run of grain as possible for the straightedge. Lay out the first rip cut parallel to the grain using a straight stick (or a carpenter's chalk line) to draw out the first cut. Make a second, parallel line ¼" wider than your desired width.

Using a sharp and lubricated 5 to 6 tpi rip handsaw, start the cut in the same manner as you did the crosscut. Orient yourself so that the cutline falls between your eyes and the saw blade. Again, you want your starting kerf deep enough to capture at least two to three teeth before ramping up to full-length strokes (and moving your thumb away). With the rip saw's coarse teeth, you may find that you need to lay the blade down almost parallel to the face of the board to start the cut without jamming. Because of the different configuration and cutting action of rip teeth, you'll also find that the most efficient cutting angle will be steeper than that of the crosscut saw — about 60°. If the cut wanders away from the cut line, use the same trick of laying the saw down and reestablishing a kerf parallel to the line. If you feel the cut slowing down, stop and re-lubricate the saw with paraffin or a squirt of vegetable oil.

Now take the strip to your workbench and use a try square to draw a perpendicular crosscut at each end of the board. Come in at least 1" from the original end cut of the board — even more if there are any splits here. Secure the board against a stop (mine swivels up at the end of my bench) and crosscut each end using a panel saw.

I lay out a straight cutline along the length of a clear, straight-grained 4/4 board with a straight stick. Because I may make the line run parallel to the grain, the cutline won't necessarily run parallel to the edge of the board.

When I have trouble starting the cut with a coarse rip saw, I'll lay the blade down almost parallel to the face of the board to get the kerf started.

Ripping the board to the layout line. The saw blade runs freely between the two top planks of the sawbenches — the inner legs of the horses are nearly vertical and are out of the line of the cut. Note that I'm holding the saw at about 60° to the face of the board — the most efficient cutting angle for rip-filed teeth.

Here I'm laying the saw down to the cut line to re-establish a tool track that will correct the direction of the saw cut.

I use my shop-made try square to make a line at the desired length.

Because this is such a short cut, I crosscut the workpiece to length at my bench using a panel saw (a short-bladed handsaw). Note that I'm utilizing a couple of holddowns and the flip-up stop on the bench to fully secure the board (allowing my attention and energy to focus on sawing to the line).

AT END OF STROKE, FORWARD HAND IS ONLY PUSHING; REAR HAND IS PROVIDING DOWN FORCE TO KEEP SOLE REFERENCED TO EDGE

AT BEGINNING OF STROKE, YOU MUST KEEP SOLE REFERENCED TRUE TO EDGE OF BOARD; FORWARD HAND MUST PROVIDE FIRM DOWN-PRESSURE — REAR HAND ONLY PROVIDES HORIZONTAL PUSHING FORCE.

FORCES ON TRY PLANE TO MINIMIZE MAKING CONCAVE SURFACE

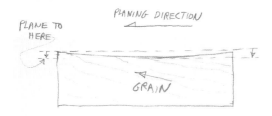

PLANE TO HERE

PLANING DIRECTION

GRAIN

* ORIENT BOARD SO CONCAVE EDGE IS UP.
* PLANE IN THE DIRECTION THE GRAIN OF THE WOOD EXITS THE EDGE.

ORIENTATION OF A BOARD FOR EDGE PLANING — CONCAVE SIDE UP; GRAIN RUNOUT IN DIRECTION OF PLANING

3. True One Edge Using a Long Try (or Jointer) Plane

These planes are, respectively, 22"- and 24"-long. The trick to creating a perfectly straight edge with any handplane is to allow it to do its job. This means that you have to handle the tool so that its cutter is always allowed to refer to the sole of the plane with an even amount of pressure. Whenever you push down too hard on an unsupported end (typically the back of the plane at the beginning of the cut and the front of the plane at the end of the cut) you make the blade cut deeper than it should at those times, creating a gently convex, rather than a perfectly straight,

With the board oriented on its edge and wedged into a stop (I'm using the shop-made fixture you will build — you could simply clamp it in a vise for now), I plane the edge perfectly straight with a 24"-long try plane.

cut along the length of the board. This is why all books and teachers tell you to push down on the front of the plane at the start of the cut and on the back of the plane at the stroke's end as you exit the board.

Begin by sighting along the edge of the board to see what you are going to be dealing with. If the edges look fairly straight, choose either one to plane true — otherwise choose the one that appears to be concave along its length. It's much

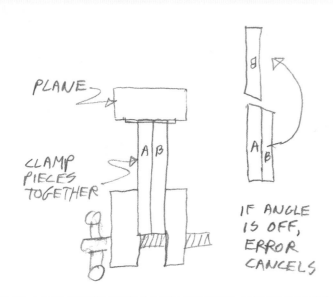

PLANE

CLAMP
PIECES
TOGETHER

A | B

A | B

B

A | B

B

IF ANGLE
IS OFF,
ERROR
CANCELS

MATCH JOINTING

If you are planning to rip your stock to thickness, you can employ a technique known as "match-joining" to test and correct the straightness of the edge. After jointing the edge, resaw your stock in half and then hold the trued edges together. If the edges are perfectly straight, there will be no gaps anywhere. If not, the error will be magnified by a factor of two. To correct any error, clamp the two pieces together and plane both edges at once to remove the high spots. Then unclamp and test the edges against each other again. You can achieve an accuracy of plus or minus .005" with this method.

easier to plane down the ends to meet the valley in between than it is to change a mountain into a valley! Also orient the board so the grain is running out along the edge in the direction you will be planing it (see the top drawing on page 85). If you can't see the grain runout, you can often feel it by running your finger along the corner of the board. Sometimes you won't know it until you actually plane the board — it will plane more smoothly and easily in one direction than the other.

Now set the plane to take a fairly coarse (like thick paper) shaving. Start planing the edge between the ends, working your way out to either

To check my progress, I simply tilt the plane and sight under it for gaps or to see if it rocks (indicating a high spot). If there is a gap, I take a few strokes at either end to bring them down — if there is a high spot in the middle, I focus some strokes here. In each case, I'll finish up with a few full-length strokes, checking to be sure that the plane produces a full-length shaving.

To check to see if the edge is square to the face, I slide a small square along the length of the edge. If it's off, I'll correct the angle with the plane in that area, and then finish with a full-length stroke.

---

end as you progress until you are making full-length shavings. Check your progress by holding the corner of your try plane against the edge and look for high spots. If a gap shows in the middle, the ends are high; if the plane pivots, it's indicating a high spot. In either case, take a few strokes on the high spots and then carefully shoot the entire length of the board and test again. When you feel you have it, check the full length of the edge against a known straightedge such as a millwright's straightedge or the bed of a planer. You can also test the edge through "match-jointing" as described at top left on page 86.

To remove the board from the fixture, I tap against the wedge with the handle of the mallet. I've carved an indentation in the wedge for just this purpose.

A quick check to see if the edge is straight is to see if it rocks when set down on the flat bench. If the edge is hollow, it will show a gap in the middle.

4. Flatten and Smooth the Faces

If your stock isn't already at ½" thick or less, this is the time to either plane it down (by hand or by machine) or to resaw it to that size on a band saw. I prefer the latter as it wastes less wood and I'll end up with a piece of stock for match-jointing and for making a second straightedge!

Using a jack plane with a well sharpened and slightly cambered blade (so the edges don't dig in), remove the saw or machine marks and flatten both faces of the board. Run the plane from one end to the other, overlapping the strokes as if mowing a lawn. Stop as soon as the plane produces full-length shavings. If the plane seems to bog down halfway through the cut, back the blade off a little bit to take a less-thick shaving. To bring the surface to a mirror-smooth finish, you can make the last few strokes with a smooth plane that has been freshly sharpened. Remember to sweep the bottom of your planes over a wax block or oiled carpet scrap to reduce friction after every dozen or so strokes.

If I began with 4/4 stock, I resaw it in half on the band saw.

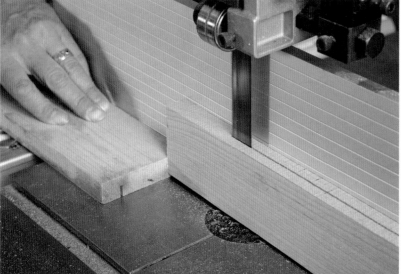

For safety, I use a sacrificial stick to push the board as I near the end of the cut. I stop pushing as soon as the blade exits the board, then step around to the other side of the table and pull the board the rest of the way through. (A roller stand, not shown in the photo, supports the board past the end of the table.)

With the board captured between the tail vise and bench dogs, I use a jack plane to remove the saw marks left by the band saw blade.

To keep the plane running nearly friction-free, I constantly stroke its sole across a piece of carpet infused with camellia oil.

I switch to a smoothing plane to create a mirror-smooth surface. Note that I've marked across the board with a wax pencil so I can observe my progress.

To create a curved edge, I mark out the centerline apex and the end points on the board. I then set brads at the end points and clamp a pointed stick at the apex and spring a thin batten to the curve. Note that the handle of the block plane is bearing against the protruding end of the batten — this "fairs" the curve by preventing the stick from straightening out between the apex and the end point.

5. Layout a Long Curve Along the Other Edge

Why put a curve or taper on one side and on the ends of a straightedge? Well, it looks nice for one thing, but there are two other good reasons: The shape automatically refers you to the trued reference edge of the tool, and the reduction of wood at each end of the board serves (theoretically at least) to reduce the tendency of the board to bow over time because there is less wood at the ends of the board to change dimension. To lay out the curve, use a thin square of wood (about $\frac{3}{16}$" $\times$ $\frac{3}{16}$" and a foot longer than the straightedge) as a drawing batten. Set a tall finish nail at each end to define the amount of curve. Push the batten against the two nails and push the center to the apex of the curve at the centerline with a small stick and clamp it in place. Draw along the outside of the batten. I use a long French curve drawing template (called a ship curve) to complete the shape of the curve at each end. If you don't have a set of these curves, you can make a very simple drawing bow (page 167) with a thickness-tapered stick that can be adjusted to a wide range of curves of constantly changing radius.

To complete the curve, I pull out the brads and use a long French curve as a template to create a pleasing conclusion at each end of the straight edge.

6. Shape the Curve

Use a drawknife (or a hatchet if you want to live a bit more dangerously!) to quickly remove waste material to within ⅛" of the layout line. Lay the board on its side and trim and smooth to the line with a block plane. Try to keep the sole just ahead of the blade always contacting the wood to create a reference and bearing surface. You know you have it oriented correctly when you are producing a shaving along the full length of the curve.

You may find it easier to switch to a spokeshave to smooth the tight curves at the ends of the board. Because here you are shaving mostly across (rather than with) the grain of the wood, choose a low-angle spokeshave. Most typical metal versions have blades set at a high angle and, because of the higher back pressure, are more challenging to use to make smooth and fair cuts along end grain.

To quickly remove material near to the curve line, I set the board on its end on my sawbench and whack off the waste with a hatchet. (For the faint of heart, you could opt out of this step and drawknife or bow-saw off the bulk of the waste!)

With the board clasped upright in my shoulder vise, I waste just about to the line with the drawknife.

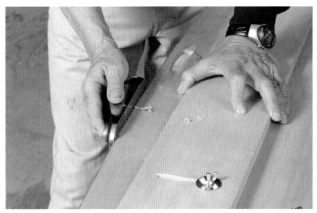

Laying the board on its side (I'm using the sticking board we'll build later — you could just clamp stops to your bench for now), I come right to the line with a block plane.

With practice, you can plane "fair" to a tight curve with a block plane if you are careful to keep the plane's sole just ahead of the blade constantly in contact with the wood.

The other option for fairing tight curves is to use a low-angle spokeshave — here I'm using a wood-handled version.

7. Bevel the Bottom Edge on One Side

To make it easier to read gaps between the straightedge and the surface being tested, it helps if its testing edge is thin — around ¼". Rather than making the whole straightedge that thin (it would be too wobbly), you can simply plane a wide bevel along one side of the straightedge. Referring to the Straightedge End View draw-ing on page 82, lay out the extent of the bevel on one face of the board and along the bottom edge using your marking gauge. Darken the cut-line with a pen or pencil as necessary. Using your grease pencil, draw lines between and connecting the layout lines so you can track your progress as you plane away the waste. These lines are clearly visible and give you ample warning as you ap-proach the extent of the taper on both the face and the edge of the board. Now secure the board between two bench dogs set below the surface of the stock. This is an example of where wooden bench dogs might be more appropriate than metal — you don't want to hit metal dogs with your plane as they will really bark up the edge of your cutter! Hold your jackplane at an angle over the bottom edge and begin to plane away the waste, continuing until you reach the layout lines.

8. Bevel All the Edges

To prevent splintering along the crisp edges of the board and to make the tool more comfort-able to handle, use a small block "trimming" plane to create a small bevel on all the corners. You'll find that "knocking off the corners" is a common task on most exposed edges of furniture components as it not only prevents splinters, it also creates a tiny facet that reflects the light and adds a little sparkle of interest to the eye.

To lay out the thinning taper along the edge of the straightedge (which will make it easier and more accurate to read when sighting under its edge) I mark its extent with a marking gauge.

I mark the area to be removed with my wax pencil.

Using a jack plane set to make a fairly coarse cut, I plane away the waste, tracking my progress by observing the disappearance of the wax lines.

9. Drill Out Hanging Holes

Using a brace and a center bit, drill a ½" hole near either end so you can hang the tool up. Another benefit of these holes is that they may further reduce the tendency of the wood to change shape over time (because there is less material to move). To prevent tear-out when drilling with a center bit, stop as soon as the center pin barely protrudes on the opposite side of the board. Turn the board around, set the pin in the tiny hole and drill in from that side. Alternatively, you could clamp on a backing block. With either strategy, you'll end up with a perfect, tear-free hole. Bevel the edge of the hole with a round file to prevent splintering.

After drawing out the handle hole, I orient a drill bit over the drawing and mark the location of the centerpoint of the bit.

I install the bit into a brace and drill both holes. To prevent a blowout, I only drill deep enough to show the centerpoint of the bit on the opposite face — I then drill in from that side, using the puncture point to orient the drill bit.

To keep the drill perpendicular to the face, I check its shank against a machinist's square.

I join the holes to create the handle cutout with a keyhole saw.

A cabinetmaker's rasp, followed by a cabinetmaker's file, makes quick work of smoothing the saw cuts.

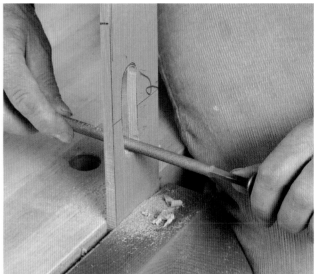

I use a round rasp and file to smooth the circular areas.

Just "for fancy," I ease the corners of the handle to a pleasant hollow by carving with a gouge.

10. Smooth the Stick

Go over the entire surface with 220- or 380-grit sandpaper on a soft rubber sanding block to remove any plane marks, scuffs and smudges.

11. Apply an Oil Finish

I use three to four coats of penetrating oil made by Bio-shield (Hard oil #9). Its non-petroleum distillate driers are very low in toxicity and fumes, yet it hardens quickly (within an hour in my 65° F shop) to a rich, in-the-wood sheen. Another low-toxicity finish that I recommend is an oil and beeswax product made by Skidmore. (Sources for these products are listed in the Resources section.) Apply these finishes with a synthetic "fine" steel wool (it looks and feels like a soft scouring pad) and then buff the final coat with a piece of wool. If you want to achieve a varnish-like sheen, continue to add thin coats — wipe the oil on and almost immediately wipe it off. I've gone up to a dozen coats on some of my work when I want to produce an incredibly rich, deep (and durable) sheen. Penetrating oil slows down moisture exchange, which in turn slows down expansion and contraction of the wood. Another option is to apply several coats of shellac after the third coat of oil has completely dried.

Using a foam brush I apply a coat of hardening penetrating oil, burnishing it into the wood with a pad of medium grit (gray color) synthetic steel wool. I'll remove the excess in just a few minutes with a clean cotton rag (which will immediately get dunked into a pail of water).

Try Squares

THE PROJECT:

While you can certainly use a typical machinist's combination square for layout work, they aren't particularly friendly to the hand, they are heavy and they can easily, if mishandled, ding the wood. In contrast, a wooden square feels soft, light and warm to the touch and is a thing of beauty to look at. The sculpted shape of the blade on these shop-made squares is not just for pretty by the way: The shape reduces weight at the end of blade, focusing the weight at the handle for better balance in hand.

In addition, for our purposes here in this book, the process of making these squares will build your skills truing edges and cutting and paring precisely to layout lines … and you'll use them for making every other project in the book! Make the small one first, adding the others as the need and inspiration arises. Worried about these shop-made layout tools going out of square due to wood movement? Well don't worry — they will on occasion! As you'll see below, however, a simple test confirms a problem, and a simple fix takes care of it.

SKILLS INTRODUCED:
Making precision crosscuts and rip cuts; chiseling and paring to a line

TOOLS INTRODUCED:
Back saw; coping saw; tenon saw; paring chisel

"Der Schreiner" (The Woodworker), by Jost Ammon — 1568

THE PROCESS:

1. Select the Wood

For the handle, almost any hardwood and grain orientation will do as long as the wood is thoroughly acclimated to your shop environment. For aesthetic reasons, you might want to choose a contrasting color from the blade stock. The latter, however, should be selected from stock of even, vertical grain to ensure stability. Cut out the wood oversized in length by at least ½" and by ¼" in width. Don't worry about getting the end cuts perfectly square at this point.

2. Size the Tongue Stock to Thickness

Because you probably won't find ¼" stock at your lumberyard, you'll need to resaw the wood for the tongue from a thicker piece of wood.

A thin board secured in place with a couple of hold-downs provides an adequate stop for smooth-planing the tongue stock.

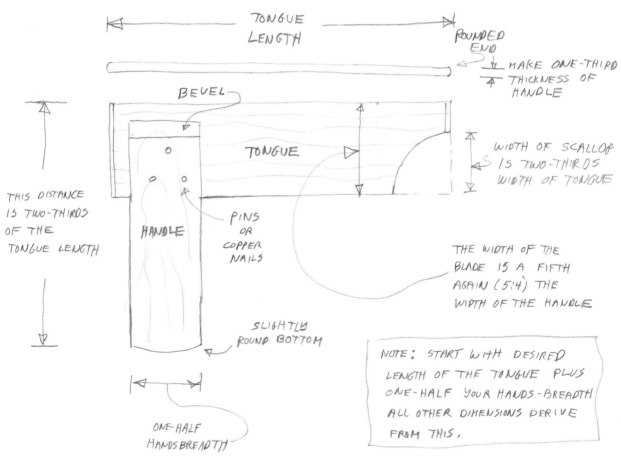

WORKING DRAWING OF A TRY SQUARE

While this can be done with a rip handsaw, it's a slow, tedious job. You could do what the 17th century joiners did and split the stock out of a bolt of wood, but that usually leaves a whole lot of planing to do, not to mention a whole lot of waste! In the 18th and 19th centuries, cabinetmaker's would use a two-man-powered frame saw with a thin and narrow blade for this purpose (at least with larger stock), but I don't expect that you'll come up with one — so let's figure on your doing this on a band saw.

You'll need to resaw the tongue stock to just over ¼" thick. Install the widest blade you can on your band saw (I use a 1"-wide blade on my saw) and set the fence to index a cut of about ⁵⁄₁₆" Now set the trued edge of the board to be resawn on the table and orient the trued face against the fence — then run the board through the blade. Change to a push stick when your hands get to within about a hand's breadth of the blade. Use your jack plane to flatten and smooth the cut face of the board by holding the stock against a thin board clamped to your workbench. Be sure to leave the board at least ¼" thick. Finally, true the remaining edges and the two ends with a block plane.

3. True the Edges and Faces

Using a sharp jack or smoothing plane, smooth the faces and then true the edges of the tongue and the handle stock straight and square to the face and parallel to one another. Use calipers to test the parallel-ness of the edges of the tongue — it has to be within a few thousandths of an inch to pass muster here. To make an adjustment to an edge, set your plane to take fine shavings and take a few strokes at the end of the board that needs to be narrowed. Now make a full-length stroke and check with your straightedge for straightness, and with calipers for parallel with the opposite edge.

4. Lay Out the Components

Using a tongue length of 8", mark the length of the handle to the proportions specified in the drawing. Leave about ¼" waste at one end of each component for final trimming.

With the tongue stock held upright in the vise at my joinery bench, I saw it to width using a 10 tpi (or ppi) crosscut handsaw. (A typical rip hand or panel saw would be overkill here — in this thin stock it would tend to jam and it would leave a very coarse kerf to clean up.)

Here I'm using my shop-made straightedge to check the edge of the tongue for true.

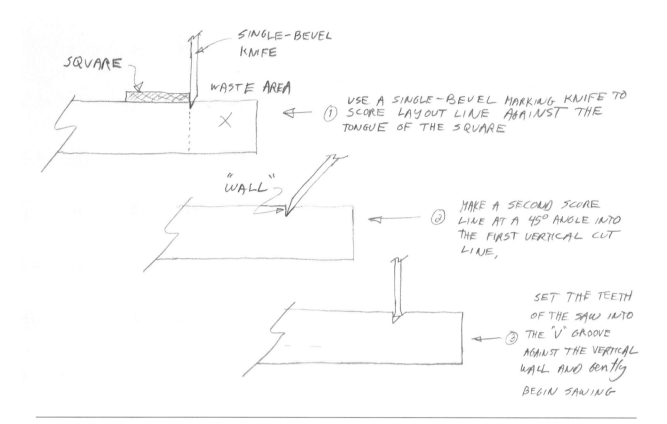

SQUARE

SINGLE-BEVEL KNIFE

WASTE AREA

X

① USE A SINGLE-BEVEL MARKING KNIFE TO SCORE LAYOUT LINE AGAINST THE TONGUE OF THE SQUARE

"WALL"

② MAKE A SECOND SCORE LINE AT A 45° ANGLE INTO THE FIRST VERTICAL CUT LINE,

③ SET THE TEETH OF THE SAW INTO THE "V" GROOVE AGAINST THE VERTICAL WALL AND gently BEGIN SAWING

MAKING A TOOL TRACK "V" CUT FOR THE BACK SAW

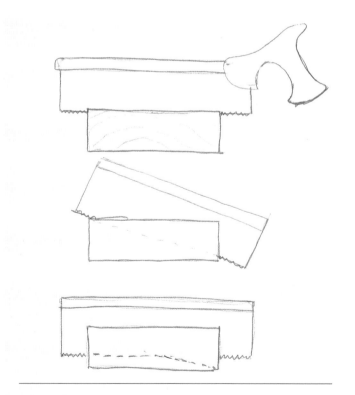

THE PRECISION SAWING PROCESS IN STEPS

5. Precision Crosscut the Components to Length

Begin by marking a square cut line at the layout marks using a sharp marking knife. Set your knife at the measurement and then slide the blade of a square to the knife. (Yes, you do need a square to make a square!) Scribe a line across the width of the board and then down each edge. Create a tool track for the backsaw by making a second cut in from the waste side of the line on the face as shown in the drawing at top. The shape of the cut will be a "V" with a perpendicular "wall" along the cut line. Now clamp the stock securely on the bench with the marked face upward and set the saw blade into the "V." Begin sawing with short, gentle strokes across the full width of the board to keep it from jumping out of the "V," lifting up on the handle to take the weight of the saw off the wood (to prevent the saw from jamming and jumping out of the kerf). Increase the length of the stoke as the blade creates a kerf, establishing its own tool track. The track should fall between the blade and your eye so you can watch the line without leaning over the saw.

The goal now is to keep your body oriented so that your arm can move smoothly back and forth, piston-like. (Note that your skills and accuracy will quickly grow if you devote some time to making numerous practice cuts to teach your body how to stand in relation to the saw to prevent deflections.) Continue with full strokes, keeping the blade engaged across the full width of the board while tilting the blade so you are cutting both across the top of the board with the blade in its tool track and down the edge facing you.

Try not to cut downward on the backside of the stock at first. When you have cut fully down the edge toward you, continue to saw as you tilt the blade back up so that it now cuts down on the far side of the stock. If you keep the blade indexed to both the face and the edge cutlines that you can see, the saw will automatically cut right to the line along the face and edge that you can't see — this is the inherent, benevolent magic of the Western-style back saw working for you!

6. Shape the Blade and Handle

With the blade now cut to width and length, lay out a curved cut-out at one corner as shown in the working drawing. The radius isn't critical, other than to leave the upper one-third of the tongue straight as is. I often use the French curves of a "gooseneck" cabinet scraper to trace a pleasing changing radius. You can also use a compass or simply find a jar lid that looks right to your eye to draw the curve. Square across the edges and draw the line on the other side.

Now secure the tongue flat on the bench with clamps or holdfasts, locating the curved layout line close to edge of the bench (to reduce vibration). Then cut along the line with a coping saw or a bow saw fitted with a narrow blade. Orient the blade so that it cuts on the downward pull stroke. Cut to within 1/16" of the line on both sides and then use your half-round cabinetmaker's rasp and file to shape the curved edge to the line. Just for looks, I apply the same curve to the bottom end of the handle, following the same process — though I wait until after I've cut the bridle joint to do this.

With the stock held securely to my bench, I cut to the curved line with a coping saw. The teeth are oriented to cut on the down stroke.

To lay out the decorative curve at the end of the tongue, I'm using a curved cabinet scraper and choosing a section of changing radius that looks good to my eye.

I smooth up the curve with a cabinetmaker's file.

On the straight end grain, I use a flat file to smooth and gently shape it by giving it a slightly elliptical cross-section.

To ensure that the two edges of the tongue are precisely parallel, I measure their width with a caliper at each end of the board. I'll trim one edge as necessary until I get them parallel within a couple thousandths of an inch.

With the tongue held in a bench hook set on my joinery bench, I cut the tongue to precise length with a crosscut backsaw.

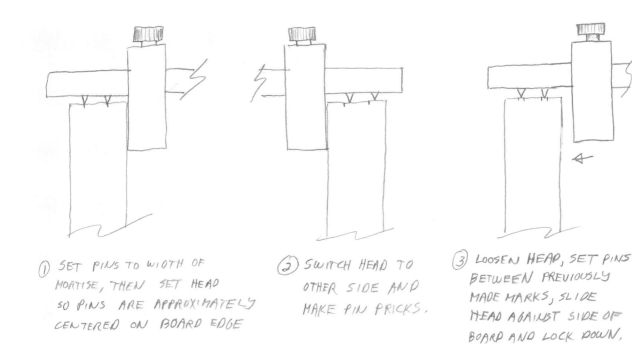

① SET PINS TO WIDTH OF MORTISE, THEN SET HEAD SO PINS ARE APPROXIMATELY CENTERED ON BOARD EDGE

② SWITCH HEAD TO OTHER SIDE AND MAKE PIN PRICKS.

③ LOOSEN HEAD, SET PINS BETWEEN PREVIOUSLY MADE MARKS, SLIDE HEAD AGAINST SIDE OF BOARD AND LOCK DOWN, MORTISE LAYOUT IS NOW CENTERED ON STOCK.

SEQUENCE SHOWING HOW TO CENTER MORTISE PINS ON A BOARD EDGE

7. Lay Out the Bridle Joint

Laying out a bridle joint offers an excellent excuse for learning to use a mortise gauge with tool slaving! Begin by marking the extent of the slot to receive the tongue along the handle as indicated in the working drawing. Note that the top edge of the tongue extends past the end of the handle, allowing you to trim the top as necessary to maintain a perfect 90° angle. Now set the pins of the mortise gauge to the width of your ¼" chisel (remember that you made the tongue stock a bit thicker than ¼" — you'll later plane it thinner to fit the completed slot of the bridle). To center the slot along the edge of the handle, eyeball the centerline and index the mortise gauge head first to one face of the handle, then the other, making a mark each time with both pins. The exact centerline falls between these marks — so back off the head, set the points between the marks, move the head back up against the stock and lock it down. Now run the points up one edge from the cross-edge mark, across the end and down the other side to the other cross mark. Use your marking knife to deepen the lines and to make a V-cut across the

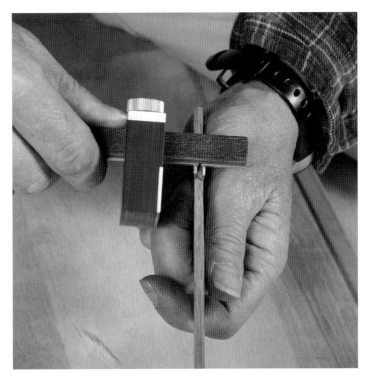

To layout the bridle joint that will accept the tongue, I set the dual pins of a mortise gauge to the width of my ¼" chisel — which is slightly narrower than the thickness of the tongue stock.

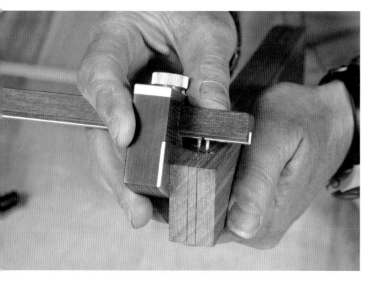

After centering the dual marks on the edge of the handle stock I scribe the cutline for the bridle, starting and stopping at a layout line indicating the depth of the bridle joint.

I make the cut using a tenon saw, beginning by gently cutting all the way across the end of the board with the blade inserted into the V cut I made earlier with a marking knife.

Tilting the blade upward as I go, I cut along the facing edge of the board, trying to split the cutline until I reach the bottom layout line.

To finish the cut, I simply tilt the blade back up as I continue to cut, being careful to keep the blade registered against its previously cut kerf. With practice, you'll find that the blade will automatically transfer the cutline on the front edge to the back, making a joint line that will need little if any paring to fit.

end grain. (Don't try to make a V along the grain on the sides of the stock — its difficult to do with accuracy. Instead, darken these lines with a pencil or fine-point pen.

8. Saw Out the Cheeks

To saw down the bridle's cheek layout lines, set the handle upright in your vise (but angled a little away from you) and place a light to shine across the layout lines at a low angle so you can clearly see them. Using your rip-filed tenon saw, follow essentially the same process for precision crosscutting presented above in Step 5. Begin the cut by placing the blade in the V across the end of the board; make a few gentle strokes to start the kerf going across and then continue cutting along the front edge down to the cross mark while keeping the blade engaged across the full width of the board; then tilt the blade up as you continue stroking the saw, using the just-cut kerf as a tool track to guide the saw as you cut the far edge of the joint. Be sure to look behind the board as you are in the final stages of the cut so you won't cut past the far cross mark. Then turn the stock around in the vise and cut along the other cheek line.

9. Remove the Waste

You can remove most of the material between the cheek cuts by cutting it out with your coping saw. Slide the blade down one of the kerfs to the bottom; lift it back up about ¼" and start to stroke back and forth, turning the blade into the waste. The trick is to keep the blade moving as you rotate it, otherwise it will tend to jam. In just a few strokes you will have cut to the other cheek line and released the bulk of the waste.

If your tenon saw makes a kerf thinner than your coping saw blade, the coping blade will mar the sidewall of the kerf and will be difficult to turn at the bottom of the cut. In this case, instead of fretting about your coping saw, you will find it easier to cope with a fret saw. (Puns intended). If you don't have a fret saw, you can make a series of cope cuts as shown in the drawing at right.

To remove the remainder of the waste, get out your ¼" paring chisel and mallet. Set the stock down on your bench (it's a good idea to protect the bench with a scrap of wood) and secure it in place with a hold-down. Position the tip of the chisel to remove about half the remaining waste and tap it down about halfway through the stock. Reset the tip to remove half again and

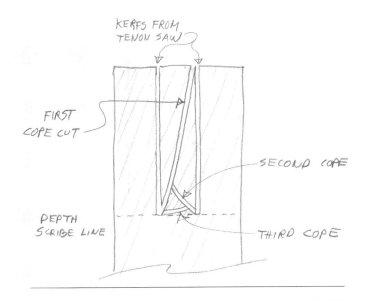

CUTTING OUT WASTE WITH A COPING SAW — THREE STEP PROCESS

After cutting both vertical lines, I remove nearly all the waste between with a fret saw.

I chop and then pare right to the line with a chisel sized to the width of the cut (or slightly under). To prevent the chisel from "blowing out" the far edge, I come in halfway from one side, then turn the stock over and finish up the cut.

I use a square to test the bottom of the cut for square — I'll pare the bottom as necessary until the protruding tongue of the square touches the layout on each edge without forming a gap.

To pare the sides of the bridle joint to fit the tongue stock, I use a float or a cabinetmaker's rasp, testing the fit after every few strokes.

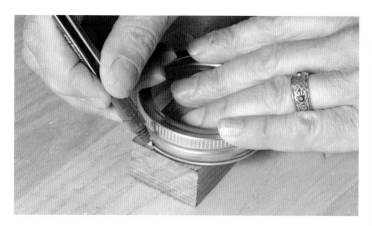

For a decorative touch, I often curve the bottom of the handle, laying it out to a radius similar to the radius at the end of the tongue. Here a jar lid is close enough!

repeat. Continue until you are within ¹⁄₁₆" or less of the scribed cross mark, then set the chisel in the mark. Position yourself so you can see that the chisel is vertical (you can set a square in the background for reference) and then tap down halfway through the stock. In most cases, the chisel — being wedge-shaped — will automatically slightly undercut the base of the joint. This is a good thing as you don't want a high spot under the tongue. Now turn the handle over and repeat the process. Check the bottom of the bridle with a square — the tongue should touch the bottom of the cut on each side of the handle. If it doesn't pare away the high spots until it does.

10. Fit the Blade to the Handle

If you have deviated a bit from the layout lines, adjust the inside cheeks of the joint with your flat cabinetmaker's rasp or a float and then smooth with a cabinetmaker's file. (You can substitute a thin, flat hardwood stick faced with 120-grit sandpaper for these tools.) Test fit the tongue stock blade and, as will likely be necessary, plane it thinner with your smooth plane until it slides in.

I remove the bulk of the waste with a backsaw.

11. Shape the Edges

Using your trim plane, shape and soften all the edges of the handle with a slight bevel, working a stronger bevel at the top of the handle where it meets the blade (for hand comfort and appearance). If you want, you can shape a deeper chamfer to fit the palm of your hand. Also saw, rasp and then file a radius similar to the one at the end of the tongue on the bottom end of the handle for both comfort and for the sake of appearance. Finally, work a slight bevel along all the edges of the tongue.

12. Install the Tongue to the Handle

Apply thin glue to the inside of the cheeks and slide in the tongue. (Hide glue is perfect here because it doesn't swell the wood, which can interfere with assembly.) Clamp a machinist's combination square to the assembly to hold it true until the glue dries overnight. To permanently ensure against movement (and to add a decorative element), I install three rose-headed copper nails with roves (dish-shaped washers) as shown in the series of photos on page 106. The source for these nails and roves is listed in the Resources. You could alternatively choose to install three ³⁄₁₆" dowels and, if you want to get fancy, make the dowels shorter so they come below the surface of the handle on both sides allowing you to easily set a decorative inlay of contrasting wood or other material over them.

13. Test for Square

A try square isn't of much use, however, unless it is dead square. To check yours for that admirable condition, set the handle against a trued edge of a board and draw out a line indexed along the tongue and onto the face of the board. Now flip the square over and draw over the line. If the square is true, the lines should be absolutely parallel. If not, you can carefully plane the edge of the tongue until they are. Repeat the process to check the underside of the tongue — you'll want this edge square for checking the edge of a board for true.

To attach the handle to the tongue, I apply a thin film of glue to the inside of the bridle joint and then slip in the tongue. I clamp a machinist's steel square to the assembly to ensure that the two pieces are aligned perpendicular to one another.

I smooth the radius with a series of rasps and files.

I bevel the top of the handle where it meets the tongue by planing across the board with a block plane to layout lines.

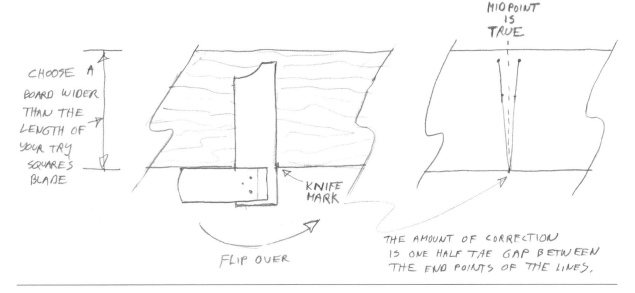

(IF THE FIRSTDRAWN LINE FALLS TO THE LEFT OF THE SECOND LINE, THE SQUARES TONGUE IS AT AN ACUTE ANGLE TO THE HANDLE.)

MID POINT IS TRUE

CHOOSE A BOARD WIDER THAN THE LENGTH OF YOUR TRY SQUARES BLADE

KNIFE MARK

FLIP OVER

THE AMOUNT OF CORRECTION IS ONE HALF THE GAP BETWEEN THE END POINTS OF THE LINES.

TESTING A TRY SQUARE

14. Apply an Oil Finish

Because your want your square to be as stable as possible over time, apply at least six coats of penetrating oil or shellac, following the process outlined earlier for the straightedge.

After the glue dries, I fix the two parts permanently together with either wooden pegs or copper rose-headed nails and roves. Here, I'm setting the roves on the nails with a punch that has had a hole drilled in its end to slip over the nail.

I clip off the excess nail shank within about 1/16" of the rove and then peen the copper shank over the rove with a brass hammer with a rounded head. This action spreads the shank slightly and then rounds it over the rove, which compresses the nail head and rove together and locks the rove in place permanently.

Winding Sticks

THE PROJECT:

To test a board for wind (twist) all you really need are a couple of sticks with two parallel edges that are longer in length than the width of the board you are testing. But what fun is that? Because it can be difficult to line up the top edges of a stick against the typically confused background of a wood shop, it works well to make the sticks from two different woods — one stick from a light colored wood and the other from a dark wood with a light colored top edge. Walnut is a good choice for the dark wood and basswood or hard maple for the light-colored stick. (Maple is the better choice for durability, though basswood is lighter, more stable and easier to work.) Make the sticks from 5/4 stock and taper them into a pyramid shape to give them more stability — and upgrade your planing skills!

To use the sticks, you set the two-toned stick on the far side of the board, centering it, and then set the second, light-colored stick closest to you. Sight the top edge of the white stick against the far stick's top strip of white using the lower portion of dark wood as a background. You will see clearly if the sticks are sitting out of parallel. (See the middle photo on page 169 of the sticks in use.) Your eye, amazingly, can detect a discrepancy to within a few thousandths of an inch.

SKILLS INTRODUCED:

Using the straightedge; jointing and edge laminating two boards; planing to make two edges precisely parallel; planing a surface to another angle; laying out, sawing and smoothing an angled end cut; applying shellac

TOOLS INTRODUCED:

Marking gauge; bevel gauge; crosscut backsaw, block plane used with backup board.

THE PROCESS:

1. Select the Wood

Because you want the sticks to stay as straight as possible, check your stock carefully to be sure that the grain is running as parallel as possible to what will be the length of the sticks. You want more than 80 percent of the grain lines revealed along the edge to run from one end to the other. Avoid sapwood and keep well away from any knots or other grain disturbances. Finally check

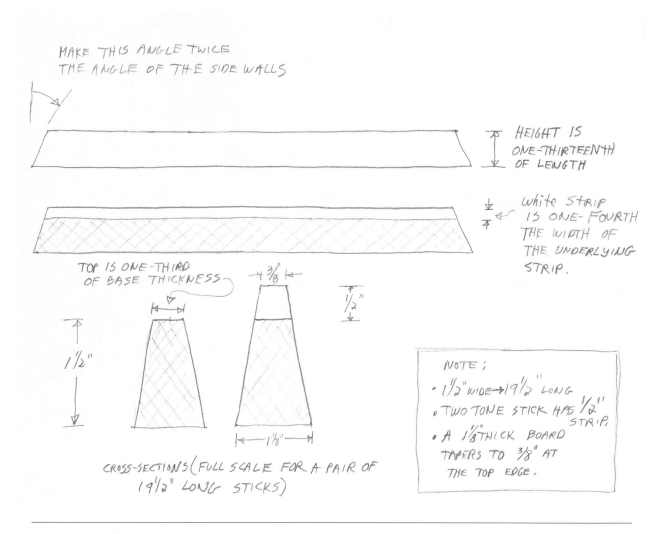

MAKE THIS ANGLE TWICE
THE ANGLE OF THE SIDE WALLS

HEIGHT IS
ONE-THIRTEENTH
OF LENGTH

white STRIP
IS ONE-FOURTH
THE WIDTH OF
THE UNDERLYING
STRIP.

TOP IS ONE-THIRD
OF BASE THICKNESS

3/8"

1/2"

1 1/2"

1 1/8"

NOTE:
- 1 1/2" WIDE → 19 1/2" LONG
- TWO TONE STICK HAS 1/2" STRIP.
- A 1 1/8" THICK BOARD TAPERS TO 3/8" AT THE TOP EDGE.

CROSS-SECTIONS (FULL SCALE FOR A PAIR OF 19 1/2" LONG STICKS)

WORKING DRAWINGS OF STICKS

the moisture content of the wood against the equilibrium table and acclimate the stock (after cutting it roughly to length and width) if necessary. Make the sticks at least one-and-one half times longer than the wood you typically work with. The width of the light-colored stick (and the dark-colored portion of the other stick) will be ¹⁄₁₃th of the stick's length.

2. Crosscut and Rip the Stock

Crosscut the stock to length, joint one edge true and then mark and rip the board to width, leaving about ⅛" for planing. When working with smaller stock, I find it easier to hold the board upright in the bench vise with the waste area positioned past the end of the bench. I use a short (20" long blade), 7 tpi rip saw as it makes a finer, more controllable cut and it's lighter and easier to handle than my standard sized, 5 tpi rip saw.

Start the cut by making short strokes across the end of the board while lifting the weight of the saw off the board to prevent jamming. When you have the kerf started tilt the saw down to about a 60° angle to the face of the board as you push through the wood with full strokes. As the cutting position gets uncomfortably low, raise the wood in the vise.

3. Match-joint Adjoining Edges

An efficient way to make two sticks in which one will include a strip of different colored wood is to simply join a dark wood strip to a light colored one. When the glue dries you rip the assembly in half, leaving a strip of the light colored wood attached to the dark.

Begin the match-jointing process by planing the edges of one of the boards straight and true (i.e. perpendicular to the face and parallel with one another). Use the longest plane you can handle for this — at least a 12"- to 14"-long fore plane. (A rule of thumb is to choose a plane at least half the length of the piece to be trued.) Check to see that the edge is dead straight by sighting the edge against your straightedge. You should not be able to pivot the straightedge (that would indicate a high spot in the middle) and neither should you see a gap between the ends (indicating high spots at the ends).

Check for perpendicular with a square. If the angle is off, you can adjust it by shifting the plane so that it cuts only on one side — the high side — of the edge (see the drawing below). Another solution shown in the drawing is to use a cambered blade, orienting it so the deeper portion of the cut is over the high side of the edge. In either case, when you have corrected the areas that aren't square along the edge of the board, take full-length strokes with the plane centered over the edge. Finally, check to be sure that the edges are parallel with one another by using a marking gauge as described in Step 6 below. Adjust as necessary.

After match-jointing the two edges, check the face of the boards with the tongue of your try-square — they should be in the same plane. If not, change the angle of the board clamped in the vise until they are.

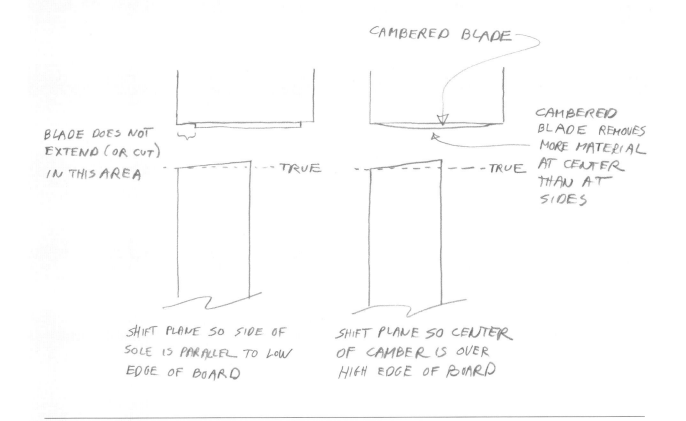

CAMBERED BLADE

BLADE DOES NOT EXTEND (OR CUT) IN THIS AREA

CAMBERED BLADE REMOVES MORE MATERIAL AT CENTER THAN AT SIDES

TRUE

TRUE

SHIFT PLANE SO SIDE OF SOLE IS PARALLEL TO LOW EDGE OF BOARD

SHIFT PLANE SO CENTER OF CAMBER IS OVER HIGH EDGE OF BOARD

ORIENTING A PLANE SO IT ONLY CUTS ON ONE SIDE OF AN EDGE — THE CONCEPT ALSO WORKS WITH A CAMBERED BLADE

I clamp up the boards on two supports that I have adjusted to be perfectly in plane with one another. Note that I've applied painter's masking tape in the area of the glue line to prevent the boards from sticking to the support.

A pair of wooden-jawed clamps are more than adequate to hold the boards together while the glue dries.

Next, plane to true the adjoining edge of the second board and test it against the first. Again, there should be no pivoting or gaps. For a quick check: Push on the end of the second board to determine if there is resistance to movement. (If there isn't much, this indicates the presence of a high spot — on either end or one in the middle.) Also check to be sure that the faces of the two boards are in the same plane by holding the tongue of your try square against them. Mark across the joint with your grease pencil to prevent gluing the wrong edges together!

4. Glue the Two Sticks Together

When you are done with the match joint, set up a clamping fixture so their top edges are parallel with one another. Do a dry clamping run to confirm that the joint is gap free and that the faces remain parallel to one another. If all looks good, back off the clamps and apply a thin film of glue (hide or aliphatic resin) to each edge. Set the boards on the fixture (apply a strip of painter's masking tape to the clamping fixture where the glue joints will lay on it to prevent sticking). If you are using three clamps, apply the first clamp in the middle and squeeze just enough to draw the boards together. Work out from the middle and place a clamp at either end. Feel with your fingers to check that the faces are even with each other. The clamping pressure should be just enough to extrude a small bead of glue on both sides of the joint. Wait until the glue is rubbery (stop if you hit liquid to avoid smearing) and then scrape it off with a handled scraper.

After the glue has become rubbery to the touch, I scrape it off using a handled scraper.

5. Rip the Lamination in Half

When the glue is dry (it's best to wait overnight with hide glue), unclamp the assembly. Set a marking gauge to the specified width of the light-colored winding stick and then run the head of the gauge along the edge of the light-colored board. The cutter or pin will indicate a parallel cutline. Secure the assembly upright in your vise (with the light colored wood held in the vise) and then rip just to the outside of the cutline.

6. Joint Edges Parallel

Remove the light colored wood from the vise and carefully plane to the cutline. This edge should come out parallel to the first edge — and it's critical that it does or the winding stick won't accurately represent the board being tested. Check by setting your marking gauge to width at one end of the stick and test at the opposite end. Adjust as necessary with your plane until the gauge reads exactly the same at each end. (You could also use calipers for this step.) Repeat the process on the stick that now contains a light-colored strip along its top edge.

To make a clear and accurate line running with the grain of the board, I use a pin-type marking gauge to mark the cutline for ripping.

I set the workpiece into the edge planing stop (captured between two bench dogs works well also) and joint the bottom of the dark-colored board.

Because the joint line between the strips must be perfectly aligned with the bottom edge (otherwise the stick would give a false reading), I check for parallel with a marking gauge. I begin by setting the pin to the line at one end of the workpiece with the gauge's head bearing on the bottom edge.

I then move the gauge to the opposite end of the stick and check the pin here — it should fall right on the joint line. If not, I'll carefully plane the bottom edge with my try plane until it does.

7. Plane Sides to an Angle

To help the sticks stay upright in use, it's a good idea to make them pyramid-shaped by shaping each side at an angle to the base. You'll plane the angle in a similar fashion to the way you tapered the thickness of the straightedge. Begin by drawing the angle on the ends of the sticks to the specifications in the drawing and then connect the lines across the top of each stick using a marking gauge. If you can't see the line, darken it with a sharp pencil or a fine pen. Also use your China pencil to mark thick lines across each face connecting the layout lines. Clamp the stick between two bench dogs using either a tail vise or a wedge inserted between one dog and the end of the stick.

To further ensure that you can see what you are doing as you plane the angle into the sides of the stick, use a sharp paring chisel to make a bevel at each end of the stick to indicate the extent of the angle (see the drawing below). Next, capture the stick between two bench dogs and use a jackplane (set the blade for an aggressive cut — preferably with a strongly cambered blade) to remove thick shavings starting near the top edge of the stick. Slow down when the bevels at the ends begin to get small. Reduce the thickness of the shavings and plane until you reach the cutline along the top edge of the stick and the end bevels have just disappeared. Repeat this process on the other side. Smooth the surfaces with a smooth plane.

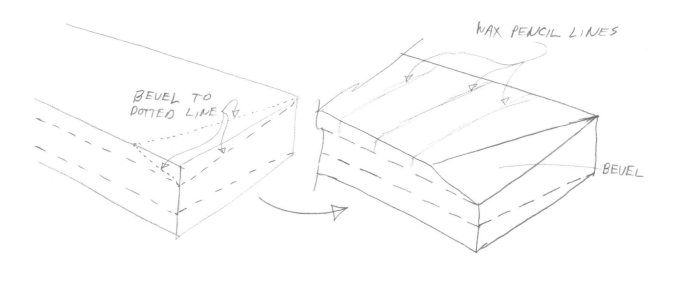

MAKING A BEVEL AT EACH END OF WINDING STICK TO DEFINE THE ANGLE CUT

By angling my ruler (the tongue of a machinist's square in this case) to read zero at one edge and 1" at the other), I can easily divide the edge into four parts by making a mark at 1/4" intervals. The one-fourth inset from each side delineates the extent of the side tapers.

To give myself a clear indicator of the material that must be removed to form the taper, I make wax pencil marks up the sides and across the top of the edge to the gauge line at the one-fourth inset.

With the workpiece captured between two bench dogs, I use a jack plane set for a coarse shaving to remove most of the waste. As I approach the bottom edge and the one-fourth inset line (I can see that the pencil lines are almost gone) I back off the blade.

If all goes well, my last stroke of the plane will remove a full length shaving that is exactly the width of the workpiece.

With the workpiece held horizontal in my twin-screw vise at my joining bench, I mark and then crosscut an angle cut with a backsaw.

Reorienting the workpiece vertically, I true and smooth the end cut with a sharp, low-angle block plane. Note the backing board used to avoid blowouts.

The lightweight and easy-to-handle trimming block plane allows me to quickly freehand a light bevel around all the edges of the workpiece.

8. Lay Out, Cut and Smooth the Ends

To lay out the end cuts, set your bevel gauge to twice the angle of the sidewalls and mark the cutlines at each end of both sticks with a knife and pencil. Use a small square to mark the perpendicular cutline on the bottom of the stick. Now secure the stick horizontally in a vise and cut to the line using your crosscut backsaw. To clean up the cut, reposition the stick upright in the vise and insert a backup board between the bottom of the stick and the back of the vise — this will prevent blowout at the exit of the plane blade. Plane the cut smooth with a freshly sharpened block plane set for a fine cut.

9. Install Centerpoint Dots

You'll notice in the photo on page 107, that each stick has a dot in the top edge of the winding stick to indicate the centerline of the stick. This gives you an instant visual reference for quickly centering the sticks on the board so the sticks will be roughly parallel to each other end-to-end. I make the dots by first shaping a ¼" diameter dowel from the dark-colored wood (see how I make dowels on page 139 in the section on making the edge-planing stop). I then cut a piece about ¼" long and glue it into a hole that I've drilled on the centerline of the top edge of the stick. I then cut and plane the dowel flush. Alternatively, you can drive in a rose-headed copper nail at the centerpoint. Make a pilot hole for the nail with your push drill.

10. Apply a Shellac Finish

Because you would like the contrast between the light- and dark-colored woods to be as dramatic as possible to make them easy to read against one another, apply a clear shellac rather than an oil finish. You can use pre-mixed, clear shellac, ready to use out of the can, applying the first coat with a natural bristle brush (shellac dissolves foam brushes). After an hour or so of drying time, I sand the raised grain with 320 sandpaper and then apply subsequent coats using a linen cloth wrapped around a golf-ball sized wad of cheesecloth saturated in shellac. This very thin coating of shellac dries incredibly fast, allowing you to recoat in a few minutes. You can remove any dust nibs in between coats by scrapping the surface with a razor blade or utility knife blade. Apply at least four coats to not only protect the wood from dirt and scuffing, but to slow down any moisture exchange that could lead to distortion.

Face Planing Stop

THE PROJECT:

Because this simple bench fixture often takes the place of vises and bench dogs for securing a board for face planing, it really speeds up the hand planing process. Most of the time a forward stop is all you need anyway especially if, like this version, the stop is wide and engages the full width of the board. And because this stop's bearing board is thin, it can secure stock down to about ¼" in thickness without getting in the way of planing.

SKILLS INTRODUCED:

Laying out the spacing of fastening holes with dividers; selecting and setting fasteners.

TOOLS INTRODUCED:

Dividers; Hand drill and push driver.

THE PROCESS:

1. Select the Wood:

The ledger can be made from any kind or cut of wood, but look for a wide piece of well-seasoned, vertical grain (quartersawn) wood clear of knots and splits to make the fixture's bearing board. Avoid plain-sawn stock because these boards are more likely to cup, producing a poor bearing surface for the leading end of the workpieces.

2. Size the Bearing Board to Length and Width and Resaw to Thickness:

When you've selected the quartersawn board, crosscut it to length and then rip it to rough width — the width of your outspread hand is about right. Surface one face flat, then true up one of the edges. Mark each of these surfaces with a squiggle to indicate they are trued reference surfaces. Mark an X on the other face and edge.

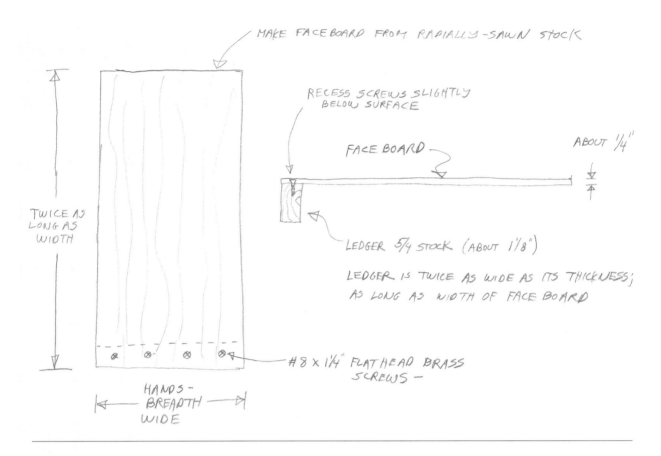

MAKE FACEBOARD FROM RADIALLY-SAWN STOCK

RECESS SCREWS SLIGHTLY BELOW SURFACE

FACE BOARD

ABOUT ¼"

TWICE AS LONG AS WIDTH

LEDGER 5/4 STOCK (ABOUT 1⅛")

LEDGER IS TWICE AS WIDE AS ITS THICKNESS; AS LONG AS WIDTH OF FACE BOARD

#8 X 1¼" FLATHEAD BRASS SCREWS

HANDS-BREADTH WIDE

WORKING DRAWING OF FACE PLANING STOP

To help ensure that the face board of the stop will stay flat over time, I made it from a piece of well-seasoned, radial-sawn stock.

Install the widest blade you can on your band saw (I use a 1" wide blade on my saw) and set the fence to index a cut of just over ¼". Now set the true edge of the board on the table, orient the true face against the fence and run the board through the blade. Change from your hands to a push stick when your hands get to within a hand's breadth (or about 1') of the blade. Use your jackplane to flatten and smooth the cut face of the board, then true the remaining edges and the two ends with a block plane.

3. Bevel the Edges:

Use your small trimming plane to bevel all the edges and corners of the bearing board. The bevels should be quite small — just enough to eliminate the chance of splinters lifting or a sharp edge cutting your flesh.

4. Size the Ledger to Length and Width:

Select a piece of wood about ¾" to 1" thick × 2" or so wide (these dimensions aren't critical) and cut it to length — which you'll determine by simply holding it to the width of the bearing board you just completed. Be sure the faces are flat and parallel to one another and then true one edge. Mark this edge with a squiggle — this is the edge that will be fastened to the bearing board.

5. Lay Out and Drill Fastening Holes:

To lay out the holes for the fasteners that will attach the bearing board to the ledger strip, begin by using your marking gauge to indicate half the thickness of the ledger board on the upper face of the bearing board. See the drawing below to see how this is done in three simple, intuitive steps. Scribe the line along the face using its end as the reference edge.

The next step is to use a set of dividers to space out and mark the position of the four screws that will hold the bearing board to the ledger. Rather than measuring and using the division of a number to get the spacing, we will employ the ancient classical order system of proportions to quickly come up with a pleasing and even spacing. Working along the line scribed by your marking gauge, adjust your dividers so it will span the width in five steps. The first and fourth stations will be the outer two holes for

By convention and by habit, I mark the trued edge and face of a board with a squiggle and mark a squared corner with a partial square.

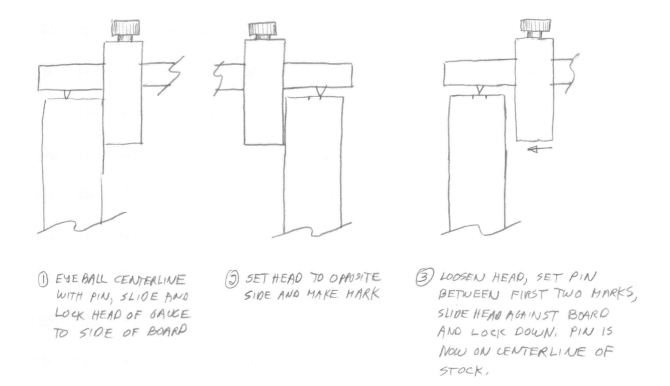

① EYEBALL CENTERLINE WITH PIN, SLIDE AND LOCK HEAD OF GAUGE TO SIDE OF BOARD

② SET HEAD TO OPPOSITE SIDE AND MAKE MARK

③ LOOSEN HEAD, SET PIN BETWEEN FIRST TWO MARKS, SLIDE HEAD AGAINST BOARD AND LOCK DOWN, PIN IS NOW ON CENTERLINE OF STOCK,

FINDING AND MARKING A CENTERLINE WITH A MARKING GAUGE — THREE STEPS

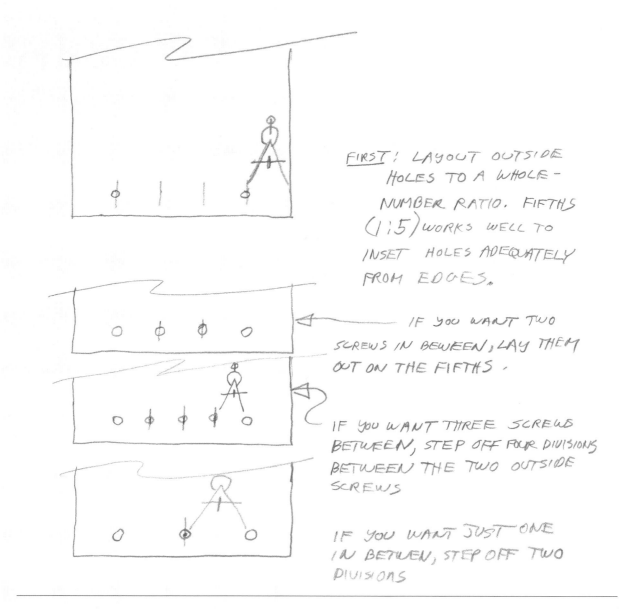

FIRST! LAYOUT OUTSIDE HOLES TO A WHOLE - NUMBER RATIO. FIFTHS (1:5) WORKS WELL TO INSET HOLES ADEQUATELY FROM EDGES.

IF YOU WANT TWO SCREWS IN BEWEEN, LAY THEM OUT ON THE FIFTHS.

IF YOU WANT THREE SCREWS BETWEEN, STEP OFF FOUR DIVISIONS BETWEEN THE TWO OUTSIDE SCREWS

IF YOU WANT JUST ONE IN BETWEN, STEP OFF TWO DIVISIONS

USING CLASSIC ORDER THEORY TO SPACE OUT FASTENING HOLES

the fasteners, so push the dividers in at these positions to mark them clearly. Now reset the dividers so that you can span between these two stations (1 and 5) in four steps. The three points in between mark where you will drill for the middle three screws. This whole process takes less than a minute and eliminates errors arising from reading and transferring measurements. The pin-pricks from the dividers also serve as pilot holes for predrilling the shaft holes for the screws.

6. Screw Faceboard to Ledger:
Though sheetrock screws are ubiquitous in the woodworking trade, they really aren't appropri-ate for fastening wood to wood because they are brittle, break easily when over-driven and they easily rust. I use square-drive woodscrews, which have thicker shanks and are made from less brittle alloys. Square drives don't strip as easily as do Phillips and the bronze color of these screws is far more appealing than the dull black of sheet-rock screws or the shinny silvery zinc of the typi-cal hardware store alternative.

Drill a hole sized to the shaft of the screws and then use your chamfer bit tool (handled or brace bit) to create a countersink for the screw heads. Next, put a thin film of glue on the ledger's squiggle-marked edge and clamp the ledger to the

After drilling the shank holes for the screws, I use a handled taper-bit tool to create a countersink for the screw heads to ensure they will set below the surface of the faceboard — and therefore out of the way of over-shooting plane blades.

faceboard. Make sure the squared edge of the face-board is aligned with the back face of the ledger.

Set the assembly aside to dry for a few hours, then unclamp and drill pilot holes for the thread portion of the screws through the shaft holes and into the ledger to the depth of the screws. You almost always want to pre-drill the full length of the screw so that the threads don't have to pull the screw through, adding stress and potentially weakening the bond between the screw and the wood. To avoid overdriving the screws (as you might with an electric driver), install the screws with a push drill or a small brace (6" to 8" swing) fitted with a driver bit. Be sure the screw heads set below the surface of the board — this keeps them out of the way of your plane blades.

7. Apply an Oil Finish

Apply three to four coats of oil, allowing about 12 hours between coats. This amount of oil will help keep the fixture from getting dirty and will slow down moisture exchange, which in turn slows down expansion and contraction of the wood.

Using a push-driver, I install the screws. For final setting, however, I twist, rather than push, the driver so I can better control the torque and avoid over-driving and potentially stripping the threads made by the screws in the wood.

Bench Hook Pair

THE PROJECT:

The bench hook is probably the most essential accessory for a workbench that has ever been invented — and that you will ever build. Essentially an instant clamp, it makes cutting small stock on the surface of the bench not only doable, but also nearly as fast and efficient (and far safer) as using a chop saw. Note that a pair of bench hooks is appropriate if you often work with stock longer than a foot or so (in other words, you make furniture and not just jewelry boxes!). Set the bench hook(s) on the bench and you have an instant backstop for holding a narrow piece of wood securely with one hand so you can cut it to length (or cut the shoulders of a tenon, etc.) with a backsaw held in your other hand. The hook's backstop keeps the board from slipping while the base protects your benchtop. Sandpaper strips on the bottom of the bench hook help prevent shifting so you will rarely find the need to clamp the fixture with a tail vise or holdfast.

SKILLS INTRODUCED:

Six-squaring a wide board (planing the stock flat and true on all edges); using winding sticks; accounting for wood movement when attaching components cross grain; cutting a dado and a rabbet; shaping a curve along the length of a board.

TOOLS INTRODUCED:

Winding sticks; straightedge; scrub plane; shoulder plane, router plane; crank-necked chisel.

THE PROCESS:

1. Select the Wood

For the face boards, pick out a piece of 1" thick (5/4) quartersawn stock that is as vertical grained as possible — I use locally available, clear vertical grain (CVG) fir or hemlock. If wide, vertical-grain stock is hard to come by in your area, you can use plain-sawn lumber of a stable, soft hardwood such as alder. Since it still might cup a bit, be sure to orient the board heart-side up (see the drawing on the top of the next page). That way, as the board dries out, it will cup downward, preventing rocking. Choose 5/4 hardwood for

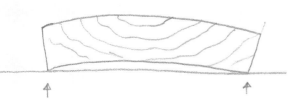

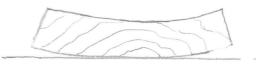

WHEN A PLAIN-SAWN BOARD
DRIES, IT CUPS AWAY FROM
THE HEART, SO THE EDGES
STAY IN CONTACT WITH
AN UNDERLYING SURFACE

IF HEART-SIDE DOWN
THE BOARD WILL ROCK
IF IT CUPS

EFFECT OF DRYING ON A PLAIN SAWN BOARD; WHY HEART-SIDE UP PRODUCES A MORE STABLE BENCH HOOK

In this side view, you can clearly see the construction of this deceptively simple fixture. The backstop — featuring a curved back for hand comfort — is set into a rabbet while the ledger is lightly rabbeted and set into a dado.

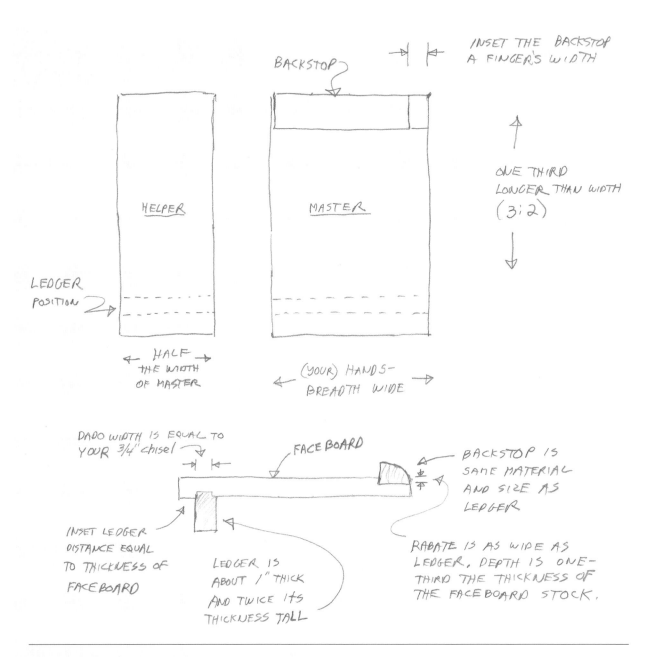

BACKSTOP

INSET THE BACKSTOP
A FINGER'S WIDTH

HELPER

MASTER

ONE THIRD
LONGER THAN WIDTH
(3:2)

LEDGER
POSITION

← HALF →
THE WIDTH
OF MASTER

← (YOUR) HANDS-
BREADTH WIDE →

DADO WIDTH IS EQUAL TO
YOUR 3/4" chisel

FACEBOARD

BACKSTOP IS
SAME MATERIAL
AND SIZE AS
LEDGER

INSET LEDGER
DISTANCE EQUAL
TO THICKNESS OF
FACEBOARD

LEDGER IS
ABOUT 1" THICK
AND TWICE ITS
THICKNESS TALL

RABATE IS AS WIDE AS
LEDGER, DEPTH IS ONE-
THIRD THE THICKNESS OF
THE FACEBOARD STOCK.

WORKING DRAWING OF BENCH HOOK PAIR

the ledgers and for the backboard — the grain orientation isn't critical here.

2. Six-square the Faceboards

Cut the faceboards to length and then to width as shown in the working drawing. Notice that there are no measurements: you'll simply step out whole-number proportions with a divider. The next step is to "six-square" the boards. This is a process in which you plane each face flat and parallel to one another, and true the two side edges and the two ends so they are square to

both faces and parallel to each other. The "Six-Square Process" is shown in detail on page 169.

3. Optional: Rough up the Faces

To help keep workpieces from slipping around on the bench hook's faceboard, you might want to rough up the surface a little bit. You can do this by running very coarse sandpaper (80 grit or even coarser) across the grain. You can also do the job with a toothed blade installed into a low-angle jackplane.

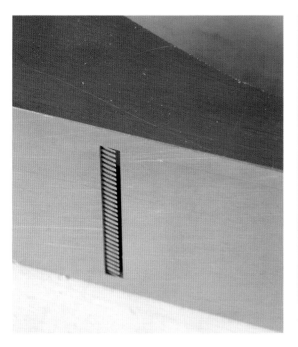

A toothed blade installed in a low-angle jack plane.

The toothed blade will produce a series of ridges across the surface of the wood, creating a rough, high-friction surface that helps keep material from sliding around.

4. Size the Ledgers and Backstop

Cut the backstop and ledger to the proportions specified in the drawing. Now cut the backstop to length. Because the length of the ledgers is simply the width of your faceboard stock you can skip taking the extra step of measuring (i.e. coming up with a number) and simply hold the ledger stock to your faceboard and mark the length directly. Wait, however, to cut the ledgers to finished length until you have worked a rabbet along the edge that will fit into the dado

on the underside of the faceboards. Go ahead, however, and cut the length of backstop to the width of the faceboard minus about a finger-width ¾" to 1". (This will create an inset on one side (the right if you are right-handed) so you can make crosscuts over the faceboard, protecting your bench.

5. Lay Out the Rabbet for the Backstop

Creating a rabbet for the backstop to nestle into isn't entirely necessary if you are only going to

To mark the length of the back stop, I hold it directly to the faceboard and make a tick mark with my pencil or marking knife.

To mark the width of the backstop on the faceboard to delineate the rabbet, I first set my marking gauge to the backstop.

I then transfer this setting to the faceboard, being careful to keep the head of the gauge tight to the trued end of the faceboard.

To create a registration "wall" for my backsaw, I deepen the scribe line with a sharp utility knife.

use this fixture as a bench hook — it doesn't add to the strength of the fixture. You could simply butt and fasten the stop to the face as you did with the face-planing stop. However, if you ever were to cut a kerf into the backstop to guide a backsaw at 90° (allowing the bench hook to act as a simple type of miter box), you wouldn't want to cut all the way through the backstop. With the stop set into a rabbet, the buried portion is not cut through and therefore maintains its integrity. So lets cut a rabbet!

Begin by setting the marking gauge (use the cutter, rather than the pin-type gauge when going across the grain — the line is more crisper) to define the width of the rabbet. How wide? Simply set the gauge to the thickness of your backstop, then run the head of the gauge along the end of the faceboard. This edge, by the way, must be perfectly square to the face as it is acting as the reference surface for the gauge. If the end is true, then the gauge will transfer this "truth" to the cutline. Reset the gauge to mark the depth of the rabbet — which is about one-third the thickness of your faceboard.

6. Cut the Rabbet

To provide an effective tool track for cutting the shoulder of the rabbet, deepen the shoulder scribe line with a utility knife and make a second cut from the waste side of the line in at about a 45° angle to join the line and to create

I then come in at a 45° angle from the waste area of the rabbet to create the wall.

I also scribe down to the cutline indicating the depth of the rabbet (set at one-third the thickness of the face board) to prevent the saw teeth from making splinters past the rabbet line.

a "V"-shaped "registration wall" to guide the backsaw's blade. To prevent tear-out on the back edge of the board when sawing the shoulder cut, use your knife to deepen the scribe line on the exit side of the shoulder line down to the bottom of the rabbet.

Next, clamp down a board with a squared and trued edge alongside the shoulder cutline. (With experience using your backsaw you will likely drop this step.) While holding the blade of the crosscut-filed backsaw against the guide board, saw down to the cutlines indicating the bottom of the rabbet on both the front and back edges of the board. Remove the guide board and saw a number of relief cuts in the waste area of the rabbet. If you are looking for speed and accuracy, consider adding a stop to the blade of your backsaw — this allows you to quickly cut down to the line without having to slow down as you approach the line. At the same time, the stop prevents overcutting the joint and leaving unsightly, and unfixable, saw kerfs.

To quickly remove the waste, select one of your widest chisels or a wide, shallow gouge and tap into the end grain of the board. Don't try to get out all the waste with the chisel, however, as contrary grain might cause the chisel to dive too deeply. Instead, stop chopping when there are still kerf lines visible along the bottom of the rabbet joint. Now use a rabbet plane to plane off the rest of the waste down to the layout lines. If you

I set a guide board with a trued, 90° edge to the layout line, holding it securely in place with a couple of holddowns, then use my carcase saw to make the shoulder cut.

I make a series of relief cuts with a coarser-cutting backsaw fitted with a stop. This feature allows me to saw quickly as it automatically stops the cutting action at whatever depth I set the stop. I am careful, however, to set the stop parallel to the teeth.

Working into the end of the board, I use a wide chisel encouraged with a mallet to remove most of the waste.

With only a little waste left, a rabbet plane (I'm using my block-plane version) makes quick work of bringing the rabbet precisely to the layout lines.

I trim the shoulder as necessary with a shoulder plane, indexing the side of the plane to the now-trued rabbet bottom.

To mark the width of the dado that will receive the ledger board, I "slave" the width to the chisel I will use to pare out the waste. I set the edge of the chisel to the dado's first layout line, and then give it a slight tap to make an impression across the area to be wasted.

didn't make a perfect shoulder cut with the back-saw, trim to the layout line with a shoulder plane, indexing the side of the plane to the flat bottom of the rabbet.

7. Make the Dado for the Ledger

Begin the layout of the dado by checking the width of your ledger against your selection of chisels. Choose a chisel that is about ⅛" narrower than the thickness of the ledger. You will "slave" the width of the dado to your chisel, and then slave the thickness of the ledger (by rabbeting it) to the dado, allowing you to trim it to a perfect fit.

Draw out the first cut line (inset it twice the thickness of the faceboard stock in from the edge) using a square and a marking knife on the underside of the face board. Hold the chisel upright with one edge even with the cut line and give it a light tap with a mallet — this establishes the width of the dado. Now set your marking knife to the corner of the mark left by the chisel opposite the cutline and add about 1⁄32" to allow some clearance during the paring process. Draw a second line square across the width of the face board at this point. To mark the depth of the dado, set your marking gauge to about a quarter of the thickness of the face board and scribe this dimension on the edges of the faceboard where the dado exits the board. Then square down to the gauged cutlines. You have now outlined the dado.

To ensure a precision crosscut to establish the sidewalls of the dado, again create a registration wall at both layout lines. In harder woods you may need to repeat the procedure to make the

Next, I set my marking gauge to the chisel line — but I add about 1⁄32" to give the chisel a bit of wiggle room during the paring operation. I then slide a square up to the knife blade and scribe the second cut line for the dado.

After deepening the scribe lines and cutting the shoulder kerfs with my carcase saw, I make relief cuts with my stop-fitted backsaw.

track deep enough to contain the teeth of the backsaw, preventing it from jumping out during the initial saw strokes.

Now secure the board to the workbench (usually between the dogs of a tail vise) and use your crosscut backsaw and a guide board to saw precisely down each layout line to the marking gauge depth lines. Lay the saw blade into the scribed "V" cut and gently start sawing in short push strokes. Continue cutting as you watch the vertical cutline on the edge facing you, stopping when you reach it. Cut the second side of the dado to the layout lines, and then saw two to four more kerfs between the lines, being careful not to cut past the depth lines. If you install a stop on the side of the blade, it will automatically stop the saw at a set depth. This really speeds up the process and is well worth doing when you are cutting more than one dado.

Chisel in (with the bevel-side up) from each end to about the middle of the board, tapping lightly with a mallet to remove most of the waste. To avoid over-deepening the dado, aim the chisel upwards a bit. Stop before the saw kerf lines disappear and don't worry about the high areas left behind by the chisel. You can remove the remaining waste and form a perfectly flat bottom using either a crank-necked chisel or a router plane.

Because the crank-necked chisel brings your hand up and out of the way when the blade is buried in a dado, you can make full-length strokes across the width of the board while indexing the cuts to the flat bottom of the chisel blade. With practice, you'll quickly make smooth, flat-bottom dados with this tool. Because dados are often made across the grain, you want to keep the bevel of your paring chisels, including these crank-necked chisels, as low as possible (25° or less) and as sharp as possible.

To make the bottom of the dado perfectly flat and of even depth, you can finish up with a router plane. Because the blade of a router plane is relatively poorly supported (and not particularly easy to sharpen), you will only use it for removing the last few shavings following your chisel work. Because the blade's edge is held perfectly parallel to the base of the tool, it transfers the flat reference face of the board to the bottom of the dado, making this joint as true as possible. As you

I use router plane to make the bottom of the dado smooth and of a uniform depth.

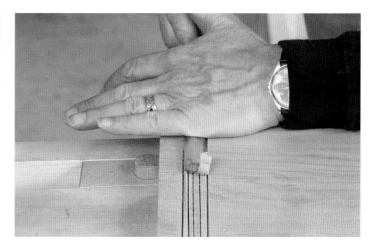

I remove most of the material with a chisel, working in from either side of the board.

The offset handle of my crank-necked chisel lifts my hands out of the way and allows me to work all the way into the center of wider boards while keeping the chisel flat to the work.

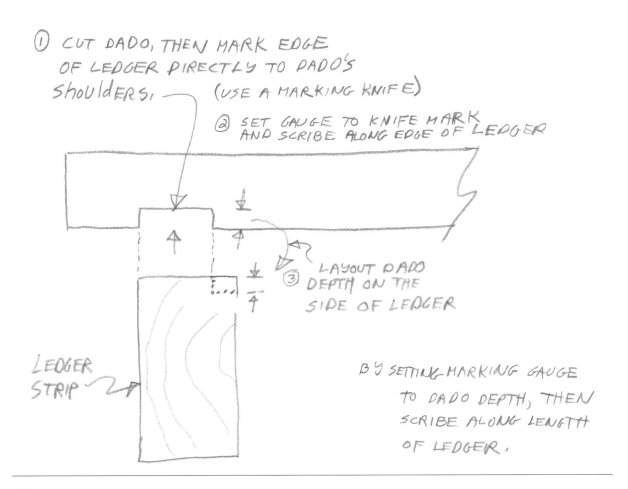

① CUT DADO, THEN MARK EDGE OF LEDGER DIRECTLY TO DADO'S SHOULDERS. (USE A MARKING KNIFE)

② SET GAUGE TO KNIFE MARK AND SCRIBE ALONG EDGE OF LEDGER

③ LAYOUT DADO DEPTH ON THE SIDE OF LEDGER

LEDGER STRIP

BY SETTING MARKING GAUGE TO DADO DEPTH, THEN SCRIBE ALONG LENGTH OF LEDGER.

LEDGER MARKED FOR FITTING TO A DADO

My try square confirms the trueness of the bottom of the dado.

To size the ledger strip to fit the dado, I hold the stock directly to the dado and mark its width on the end of the board.

work more with the router plane, you will discover other applications of this attribute, such as truing the cheeks of a tenon or the bottom or a rabbet. Repeat the steps above to form a dado on the second benchhook's faceboard.

8. Fit the Ledger to the Dado

To fit the ledger into the dado, you need to make a small rabbet in the ledger. To determine the rabbet's width, hold the ledger to the dado and mark its width on the end of the piece. To find the depth, you can use the last setting of the router plane blade to scribe a line along the length of the ledger. Otherwise, set your marking gauge to the depth of the dado and then run the head of the gauge along the length of the board.

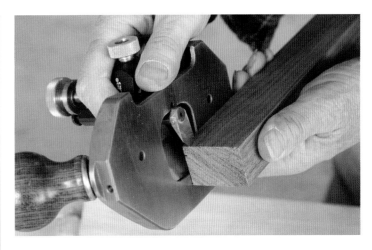

I use the last setting of the router plane's blade that cleared the dado to mark the depth of the dado along the side of the ledger.

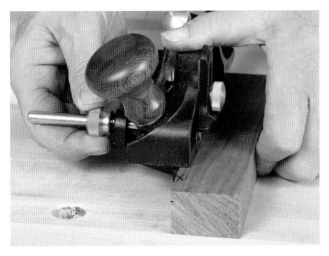

To create a small rabbet that will allow the ledger to fit into the dado, I use a fillister plane. Here, I'm setting the tool's side fence to the scribe line I made along the side of the ledger strip.

To set the depth stop on the plane, I record the scribe line that indicates the depth of the rabbet on my machinist's square

I then set the head of the square on the sole of the plane and slide the stop to touch the end of the tongue and lock it securely in place.

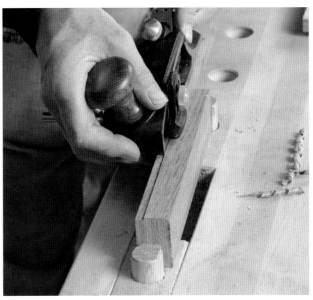

Being careful to keep the side fence indexed to the side of the ledger strip, I continue making strokes until the depth stop touches the top of the ledger.

I trim the depth of the rabbet with a finely-set shoulder plane.

Alternatively, you can set your small T-square to the depth of the dado and then run the tongue along the length of the ledeger as you hold a pencil to the end. In either case, be sure to draw an X on the waste portions with a wax China pencil.

Now set your fillister plane to cut the rabbet by setting the side fence to the scribe line and the depth stop to your machinist's square. If you don't have a fillister, freehand the cut with a medium-sized shoulder plane, stopping short of the layout line — stop when you get close and test the fit. Use your shoulder plane to adjust the rabbet in both width and depth until you achieve a snug fit. When you are satisfied with the fit, cut the ledgers to length (you'll get that dimension directly from the width of the faceboards).

With the shoulder plane on its side, I trim the side of the rabbet until the ledger slips precisely into the dado.

This is the fit I was looking for.

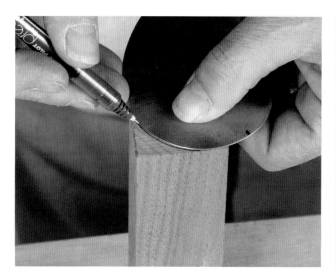

I use one of my French-curved scraper blades to lay out a pleasing (and functional) roundover on the upper back corner of the back stop.

Using my machinist's square, I draw out a line to mark the extent of the curve along the top of the back stop.

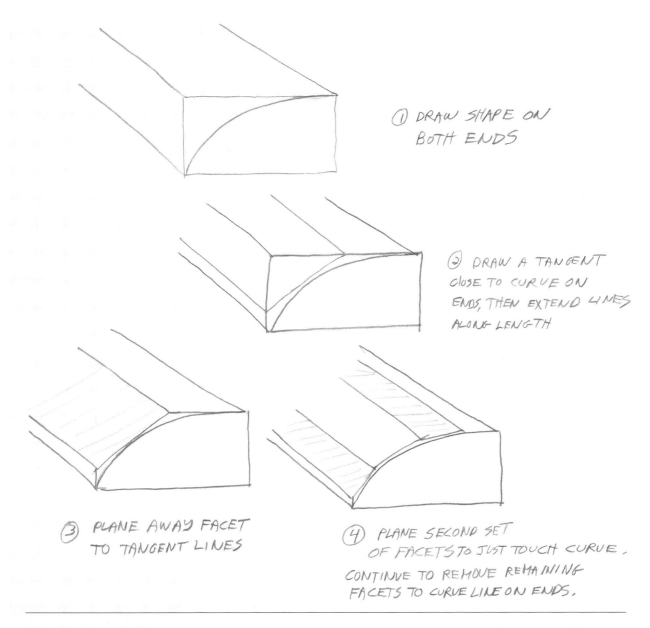

① DRAW SHAPE ON BOTH ENDS

② DRAW A TANGENT CLOSE TO CURVE ON ENDS, THEN EXTEND LINES ALONG LENGTH

③ PLANE AWAY FACET TO TANGENT LINES

④ PLANE SECOND SET OF FACETS TO JUST TOUCH CURVE. CONTINUE TO REMOVE REMAINING FACETS TO CURVE LINE ON ENDS.

LAYOUT OF A QUARTER-ROUND ON END AND EDGE OF A BOARD

9. Shape a Quarter-round on the Backstop

While not absolutely necessary, a nicely-rounded upper back edge on the backstop will be kind to your hands as you hold a board in place. Shaping a quarter-round with a block plane is also a great excuse for planing practice. The principle is simple enough, you'll make a bevel along the corner of the board tangent to the circle you marked on the end of the board to represent the quarter-round, then remove the edges of the facets until you create a round.

To lay out the quarter-round, select a circle from a drawing template (or a section of a goose-necked scraper) that represents the amount and shape of round that you want. Draw the shape on the end of the board and then draw a tangent line to the circle. Set your marking gauge (or the tongue of your small T-square) to where the tangent line intersects the face of the ledger and draw out cutlines along its length. Set the board between the dogs on your planing bench and then plane down to these lines. Next, switch to your single-handed block plane and stroke down to the edge of the facets on each face — don't bother with layout lines, freehand is accurate enough. Then plane off the edge of the second round of facets — and then the third round. If you are a stickler for removing tool marks, install a piece of 180-grit sandpaper into a soft sanding block (or the palm of your hand) and sand away, working up to 320 grit.

10. Layout and Drill Attachment Holes
Lay out the spacing of the attachment holes and drill the countersunk pilot holes following the directions given in Step 5 on page 117 for the face planing stop. Drill the holes for the ledgers in both bench stops and for the backstop in the wider faceboard.

11. Elongate Attachment Holes
Because the faceboards are much thicker than the stock we used for the face planing stop, we have to make a little change to the attachment holes to account for wood movement. You'll need to elongate one of the holes to create

To keep track of my progress as I remove the waste, I use a wax pencil to mark up the edge and across the top of the workpiece to the layout line.

A jack plane set for an aggressive cut makes quick work of removing most of the waste. The wax lines give me a clear indication of how close my strokes are to the edges of the waste area.

I use a block plane to remove the facets left behind by the jack plane, and to final-shape the curve to the layout lines I marked on the ends of the workpiece.

If I want to remove the tiny facets left behind by the block plane (though I admittedly generally don't bother), I'll use a flexible sanding block fitted with sandpaper — starting with 180 and finishing with 320.

about a 5/16"-long slot to allow the screw to slide along and allow the faceboard to shrink and expand relative to the ledger (which, due to the nature of wood, is stable in length). Without this play, the faceboard would likely split if it shrinks, or cup if it expands.

To create the slot, drill a second hole about 1/4" away from one of the holes and then make countersinks in both with your chamfering bit. Join the holes by chiseling away the waste between with a dovetail or other thin chisel. Because of the thinness of the blade, be careful to use your lightest mallet when chopping to avoid bending the blade. After chiseling, smooth the inside of the slot with a thin, flat or round file. Finally, use your chisel to join the countersink between the two holes.

To mark the inset of the fastening holes for attaching the backstop to the faceboard, I set my marking gauge to half (by eyeball) the width of the rabbet.

I then transfer this inset to the opposite side of the board and scribe the line.

To mark the location of the screw holes, I hold one leg of the divider to the edge of the board and mark the inset with the other leg. The hole made by the divider becomes the starter hole for the drill bit.

To lay out where the screw holes go — which will be an inset of one-fifth of the width of the board — I find this distance by inserting the pins of my sector into the holes on the tool's fifth calibration line. I then press the pins to each side of the face board and set my divider in the pin holes of the first calibration line. Through the magic of geometry, this distance is one-fifth of the distance between the pins at the fifth calibration line.

To ensure that the screw will slide freely, I smooth the inside of the slot with a round file.

LEFT After drilling a hole sized to the shank of the screw, I use a hand-held taper tool to make a countersink for the screw head.

MIDDLE LEFT To create an elongated hole for one of the screws (to allow for movement of the faceboard) I make a second hole about ¼" away, taper a countersink, and then join the holes by chiseling away the waste between the holes. I use one of my dovetail chisels here as the blade is quite thin — though I have to be careful to use my lightest mallet when chopping to avoid bending the blade.

---

12. Install Ledgers and Backstop

Insert the ledger strip into the dado and install the two screws. Do not, however, cinch down the screw in the slotted hole too tightly — you want to let the faceboard move as necessary. Forgo a power driver here. You'll find that driving in a screw by hand allows you to sense just the right amount of torque. Remember to inset the backstop in from one edge of the faceboard — the right side if you are right-handed.

13. Optional: Install Sandpaper for Anti-slip

To keep the boards from slipping around on your workbench, you can glue down a pair of 120-grit strips of sandpaper (or use adhesive backed sandpaper). I also add a strip of sandpaper to the bearing edge of the backstop to keep boards from slipping around. (If, however, you are going to make a kerf in the backstop to guide a backsaw, be sure to remove the sandpaper before doing so!)

14. Apply an Oil Finish

I apply about three coats of penetrating oil to this fixture to keep it clean and to help keep the boards stable.

I apply self-adhering 120 grit sandpaper to the bottom of the bench hook to keep it from sliding around on the bench.

Edge Planing Stop

THE PROJECT:

Here is another bench accessory that adds considerable speed to planing by hand — in this case, edge planing. Like the face planing stop, it fixes quickly to the bench by locking its ledger strip into a vise. Because there can be a good deal of stress placed on the ledger when planing, I recommend setting the ledger into a dado to provide plenty of shear strength. As you did with the bench hook ledger, you'll rabbet the ledger where it fits into the dado so you can easily adjust it to fit snugly — and therefore securely.

The "V"-shaped notch in the fixture's faceboard allows the stop to handle a wide range of typical stock thicknesses without any adjustment, while a light tap of the wedge holds the board securely in place. (If the board is longer than 2', you can tap down a scrap of wood under a holdfast to serve as a side-bearing surface for the workpiece.) Ideally, I'd make my stop from a scrap of 6/4 hickory — an ideal choice because its interlocking grain prevents the board from splitting when stressed. You can, though, use less tough woods by reinforcing the grain through

drilling and inserting a dowel across the grain on either side of the slot as shown in the drawing and described in the process below.

SKILLS INTRODUCED:

Crosscutting at a compound angle: drilling a long hole accurately with brace and auger bit.

TOOLS INTRODUCED:

Auger bit; bevel gauge; flush-cut saw.

THE PROCESS:

1. Select the Wood

For this project, choose a piece of plain-sawn hardwood for the face board — avoid quartersawn for this fixture as you are looking for grain toughness more than stability. Go with 6/4 stock as anything thinner will not adequately support stock upright during aggressive planing. The faceboard should be at least a hand's-breadth wide and its length one and one-half that amount.

2. Six-square the Board

See the sidebar on page 169 for instructions on this process.

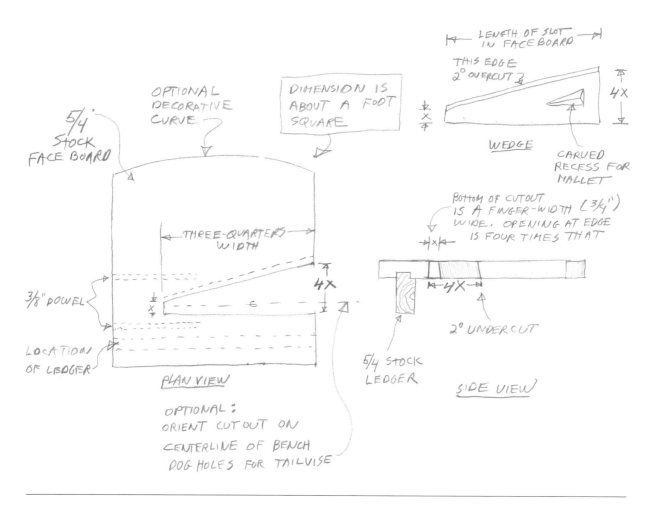

WORKING DRAWING OF EDGE PLANING VISE

The image contains the following handwritten labels:

OPTIONAL DECORATIVE CURVE

DIMENSION IS ABOUT A FOOT SQUARE

5/4 STOCK FACE BOARD

LENGTH OF SLOT IN FACEBOARD

THIS EDGE 2° OVERCUT

4X

WEDGE

CARVED RECESS FOR MALLET

THREE-QUARTERS WIDTH

BOTTOM OF CUTOUT IS A FINGER-WIDTH (3/4") WIDE. OPENING AT EDGE IS FOUR TIMES THAT

3/8" DOWEL

4X

LOCATION OF LEDGER

PLAN VIEW

5/4 STOCK LEDGER

2° UNDERCUT

4X

SIDE VIEW

OPTIONAL: ORIENT CUTOUT ON CENTERLINE OF BENCH DOG HOLES FOR TAILVISE

3. Get out the Ledger Strip

Select another piece of hardwood for the ledger strip and cut it to the same length as the width of the fixture. Use stock at least 5/4 thick. Lay out the dado to accept the ledger, making its depth a quarter of the thickness of the face stock. Inset the dado at least twice the thickness of the face board stock from the end to prevent the dado from splitting out when the ledger is put under stress during planing.

4. Make the Dado and Fitting Rabbet

Cut and smooth the dado and then make the rabbet on the side of the ledger until it fits. See the description of this process in the section starting on page 120 on making a bench hook.

5. Cut a Decorative Arc

While in no way necessary to the function of this fixture, I often like to add a little bit of visual interest to a project that I'll be looking at every time I work at my bench. For you, this bit of fancy work — shaping a gentle arc along your fixture's front edge — will provide you with a bit of practice at cutting a curve with a bowsaw.

First lay out the arc by finding and drawing out the centerline of your face board. Next, set nails at each of the side points of the arc and decide how high the arc should rise (it's purely an aesthetic decision on your part) by adjusting the string on your drawing bow. Set a nail at the apex. Hold the bow so it touches all three nails and then trace the curve along the outside of the bow. Now secure the board so it overhangs your workbench and use your bowsaw to cut close to the curved line. (If you don't have bowsaw, but you do have a band saw, then go for it!) Reset the board vertically in a vise and clean up the cut with a sharp block plane. Chamfer the curved edges with a spokeshave.

To find the center of the faceboard so I can lay out the apex of the decorative arc, I angle the ruler so that it reads an even number across the width of the board (in this case, 14"). I mark the center of the board at 7".

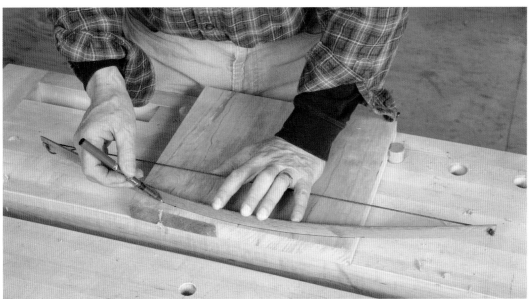

After marking the apex and the two side points, I bend my shop-made drawing bow so that it intersects the three points and then draw the cutline for the arc.

6. Drill for the Reinforcement Dowels

Select an auger bit that's about one-third the thickness of the board — that will, of course, also be the diameter of the dowels that you'll insert into the hole. Now mark a centerline along the length of the edge to receive the dowels that will run into the board to either side of the notch and make a starting hole for the screw point of the auger bit with a brad awl. Secure the board flat on the table with a pair of clamps or hold-fasts. Capture a straight length of stock under one of the holdfasts to serve as a visual drilling guide

With the faceboard held securely to my planing bench with a pair of holddowns, I use my large bow saw (fitted with a crosscut blade) to quickly cut the curve.

After marking out the location of the two dowel holes to either side of the wedge-shaped cutout, I start a pilot hole with a brad awl to orient the center-point of an auger bit.

I wrap a piece of tape around the shaft of the auger bit to give me a temporary, flag-like indicator for the depth of cut.

for the auger bit. Put a piece of tape on the bit to indicate how deep to make the holes and than drill the holes. To help you keep the auger bit level and square to the edge being drilled, occasionally check your angle by sighting the exposed bit to see that it's running parallel to the guide stick.

7. Slot and Insert the Dowels

Cut a thin slot along the length of the dowel (either pass it over a plow plane set up with a ⅛" blade or make a saw kerf with a tenon backsaw). This slot allows air to escape from the bottom of the hole ahead of the dowel and that allows it to seat fully in the hole.

Brush a thin film of hide glue on the dowel and drive it in with a wood mallet. Stop pounding as soon as the pitch of the tapping changes — that means the dowel has bottomed out. By the way, hide glue being thin, highly viscous and lacking the tendency to swell the wood, as do water-based glues, is the perfect choice of adhesive here.

8. Make the Notch

Locate the perpendicular cutline of the notch about even with the row of holes that serve the tail vise on your bench — this may come in handy if you want to use the tail vise to provide a pressure point

After securing the faceboard to the bench — and clamping down a stick to act as a visual guide for the drill — I drill out a hole with a brace and bit.

I make my own dowel by ripping out a length of stock (squared to the diameter of the hole) and then planing facets on each corner to turn it into an octagon. I make up a sticking board to hold the dowel by plowing a groove in the edge of a thick board and setting a screw to act as a stop.

With the dowel still held in the sticking board fixture, I cut a slot in the dowel that will allow the glue to flow around it, allowing the dowel to seat fully in the hole.

I orient the faceboard in my vice so that the cutline is plumb and so that the saw will clear the side of my bench. Since this cut has a slight undercut angle, I'm careful to follow the layout lines that I've made on both sides of the board.

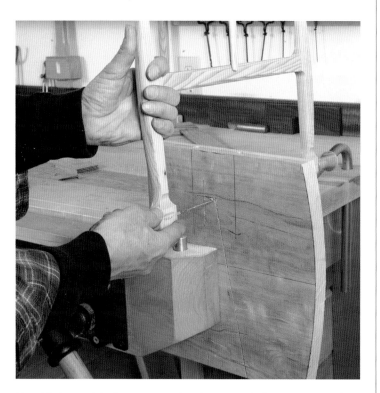

The wide frame of the bow saw provides clearance and allows me to cut off the base of the V without have to remove and reinsert the blade (as would be required by a coping saw).

against the back of a long board. Lay out the angled cutline of the notch (the side away from the vise ledger and the side that bears against the wedge) to the angle shown in the drawing. Be aware that if you make the notch more open than that, it will not grab onto the wedge very well, and if you make it less, it won't hold thicker boards.

Layout the notch to the dimensions shown in the drawing. Notice that you must also cut the angled side of the notch at a slight (about 2°) undercut. This geometry helps lock the wedge against the stock and helps keep the wedge in place. Set the bevel gauge to 3° and mark this angle at the edge of the board. Then scribe the lines of the crosscuts on both sides of the faceboard with your marking knife, darkening them as necessary with a pen or pencil.

Set the board upright in a vise with the cutline clear of the side of the bench and oriented plumb. (If you are like me, your muscles have learned how to make plumb cuts with more accuracy than angled cuts!) Use a 10- to 12-tpi crosscut handsaw to make both cuts, watching the cutlines carefully along both the top and the bottom of the face board when sawing the undercut. After making both crosscuts, connect the bottom of the two kerfs with a small-frame bow saw fitted with a narrow blade.

9. Make the Wedge
Cut a wedge from a hardwood board the same thickness as the face board. Lay it out so its angled sides run parallel with the grain of the wood. (If you cut the wedge from the board across its grain, it will quickly fall apart, which is why we can't use the wedge shaped offcut from the face board.) Remember to cut one of the sides to the same angle as the underbevel in the face board's notch. With a plane, adjust the wedge's shape as necessary so that it bears evenly against the stock when the other side of the stock bears against the perpendicular side of the notch.

10. Bevel All the Edges
Use your small block plane to work a light bevel on the edges of the fixture and the wedge.

11. Apply an Oil-base Finish
Apply oil to all the surfaces except the inside of the notch and the long sides of the wedge (you don't want to make a slippery bearing surface for the wedge).

Sticking Board

THE PROJECT:

When working wood by hand, you generally bring the tools to the wood — but when machining wood you usually bring the wood to the tools. In either case, however, you need to somehow ensure a firm connection between the wood and the tool's reference surfaces. As is typical in the hand tool realm, there are simple, low-tech solutions to this requirement, and the sticking board is a perfect example. (Though the one I show you how to build here, featuring an adjustable fence and threaded screw stops, is a bit of a fancy one.)

SKILLS INTRODUCED:

Using a bench hook as a shooting board; making a "breadboard" type mortise and tenon joint. (Note that the tenon in this case is simply created by a double rabbet while the mortise is a groove made with a plow plane.)

TOOLS INTRODUCED:

Plow plane

THE PROCESS:

1. Select the Stock

Select a minimum 4' long piece of dry, clear vertical grain 4/4 stock about 1'-wide for the base and a 4' long board half that width for the sliding fence. In my neck of the woods, this means paying through the nose for either CVG fir or hemlock. You can get away with clear, plain-sawn lumber if it's a soft (i.e. less dense) hardwood that's been thoroughly seasoned and acclimated to your shop. Orient plain-sawn stock heart-side up so any cupping due to drying will not cause the fixture to rock side-to-side.

If you are cutting the narrower board from a wide piece of stock, you can use a panel gauge (which is nothing more than an over-sized marking gauge) to produce the lengthwise cutline. If your stock has been "straight-lined" — meaning one edge has been roughly trued — set the head of the gauge to that edge. Otherwise, take a minute or so to get one of the boards edges relatively straight before using it as a reference edge. The trick to making an accurate line is to focus on watching the head of the gauge to ensure it rides consistently along the edge rather than watching the line being marked.

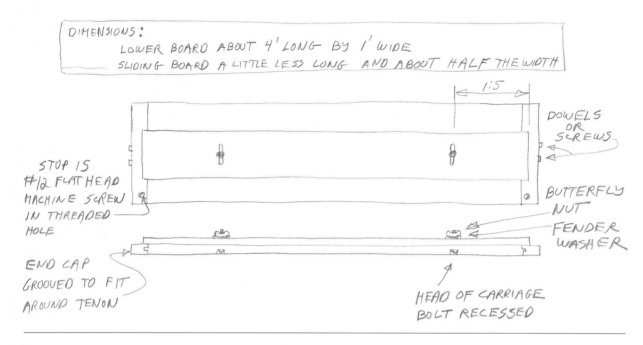

DIMENSIONS:
LOWER BOARD ABOUT 4' LONG BY 1' WIDE
SLIDING BOARD A LITTLE LESS LONG AND ABOUT HALF THE WIDTH

1:5

DOWELS
OR
SCREWS

STOP IS
#12 FLAT HEAD
MACHINE SCREW
IN THREADED
HOLE

BUTTERFLY
NUT
FENDER
WASHER

END CAP
GROOVED TO FIT
AROUND TENON

HEAD OF CARRIAGE
BOLT RECESSED

WORKING DRAWING OF STICKING BOARD

To quickly set a plow plane to the create a groove centered on the edge of a board, I first eyeball the blade at the center of the edge, slide over and lock the side fence, and make a tiny cut.

2. Get Out the End Caps and Plow a Groove

Select and rip to width the end caps for the base piece from a 2'-long piece of 4/4 cherry, maple or other hardwood. Leave it long for now. True both edges, then plow a groove along the middle of one edge using your plow plane. Begin by setting the stock upright between the dogs of your tail vise or pressed against your planing stop. Install a ¼" blade in the plow plane and adjust the tool's side fence so the blade falls in the center of the edge. Similar to the process of aligning a marking gauge to a centerline, you eyeball the center and make a small test cut from either side of the stock. The center of the groove will fall between the two test cuts. Set the depth stop on the plane to bottom out at ¼".

Start planing at the far end of the board, taking single, overlapping hand-breadth-long strokes as you work your way back to the beginning of the board. What you are doing is creating a tool track for the blade to help the fence align the blade to the edge of the board. Now work full-length strokes until you reach the depth stop. Don't worry about a little tear-out as it will be buried against the end of the base. (There is almost always tear-out with plow planes because the skate (i.e. the sole) is not as wide as the blade and cannot hold all the fibers down before they engage the blade.) Test the depth of the cut by

I then index the side fence to the opposite side of the board and make another tiny cut. I then reset the fence so the cut will fall between the two test cuts.

To ensure a perfectly square edge on the end of the board to be rabbeted, I take a few passes across the end grain with an edge trimming plane.

protruding the tongue of your T-square to ¼" and running the head along the length of the groove. It should slide smoothly from one end to the other. When you have completed the groove to your satisfaction, crosscut the stock to length (which will be the width of your base stock) on your bench hook using a crosscut carcase saw.

3. Get Out the Base

Rough crosscut out a 4' length of your 1'-wide (or so) board and then true its two edges. Square and true the ends using your low-angle jack plane followed by an edge-trimming plane if you have one.

4. Make the "Breadboard" Mortise and Tenon

Produce a tongue on each end using either your fillister plane or a rabbet plane guided by a fence. Be sure to score the shoulder of the rabbet (if not using a fillister plane equipped with a nicker) and saw the exit shoulders to prevent tear-out.

To use the fillister plane, begin by drawing the plane backwards along the length of the cut so that the nicker has a head start in cutting the fibers. Now take a series of short strokes from the far end of the board to the near end to establish a tool track. Be aware of what your hands are doing to guide the tool. The hand on the handle has the job of pushing the plane forward while the hand on the side of the plane focuses on holding the tool's side fence tight to the edge of

To determine the depth of the tongue that I'll make on the base board, I set my machinist's square to the depth of the plowed groove.

I transfer this setting to the base board, marking it with a knife.

I then slide the tongue of my combination square to the knife and scribe a line across the width of the base board.

I set the side fence of the fillister plane so the blade comes just to the scribe line.

To score the wood ahead of the blade to prevent tear-out when planing across the grain, I set the nicker ahead of the blade so that it protrudes slightly below the plane's sole.

To prevent blowout at the exiting edge of the planing action, I use a fine-toothed backsaw to sever the fibers at the layout line.

the board. It's crucially important to realize that the side fence of a fillister plane acts as the reference sole of the plane, indexing the blade upright (parallel to the fence and therefore square to the board's face) and ensuring the bottom of the rabbet will come out parallel to the face of the board. Continue planing until the tool stops cutting (which happens automatically when the stop encounters the board's face). Switch to a router plane to precisely trim the rabbet bottom on both faces until it fits the ¼" groove you made in the end caps.

5. Fit and Attach the End Caps

Now set your shoulder plane on its side against the rabbet and trim the shoulder of the rabbets true and straight, checking the fit with the end cap. When you are happy with the fit, glue the end caps in place — but only apply the glue to the middle 2" of the tongue as this allows the base to shrink and expand without splitting. To ensure the caps stay in place, you can either screw and plug them from the end (spaced about one inch to either side of center) or do as I did and drill for, and glue in, dowels.

As an alternative to the fillister plane, I sometimes use a shoulder plane to make small tongues, free-handing to the scribe line. As I go along, however, I use a square to check to be sure that I'm holding the plane perpendicular to the face of the board.

Whether using a shoulder plane or a fillister plane, I always make the last few strokes to the layout line with a router plane to ensure accuracy

If the tongue isn't quite long enough to fit fully into the groove, I'll lay the shoulder plane on its side and shave back the shoulder until the joint fits tightly.

6. Make the Stops

To make the stops for "sticking" the ends of the workpieces, you can drill and tap holes to receive ¼" 10-20 thread flat-head machine screws. This is best done in dense hardwoods such as maple or hickory. You can strengthen the wood treads in softer woods by dripping in a little cyanoacrylate. Alternatively, you can simply drill holes and in-stall threaded inserts. File the heads of the screws into a dome shape to create a sharp edge that will bite into the end grain of your work piece. (The dome shape retains the groove for your screwdriver.)

7. Get Out the Sliding Fence

Crosscut the board you ripped for the sliding fence to a length equal to the finished length of the base. Lightly bevel all the edges.

LEFT I make the height-adjustable stop by installing threaded inserts to accept a machine screw. Notice that I've beveled a sharp edge around the circumference of the screw head so it will bite securely into the end grain of the workpiece.

BELOW To make an elongated slot in the sliding fence board (so it can be adjusted side to side) I drill two holes and then connect them by cutting two kerfs with a keyhole saw.

8. Make Elongated Holes for the Holddown Screws

Lay out a pair of slots for the two 5/16" carriage bolts that will secure the sliding fence to the base. I spaced them in from each end of the fence one-quarter of the board's length. Drill a 3/8" hole at each end of the slot layout using your brace and auger or center bit — be sure to come in from each face to prevent tear-out. Connect the holes by sawing across the board with your keyhole saw and clean up the cut with your cabinetmaker's rasp and file.

9. Install the Bolts

Set the slider on top of your base (both should be oriented heartwood side up if plain-sawn) and mark the position of the slots by tracing the outline of the slots on the face of the base board. Drill a 1/8" guide hole centered between the outline marks at the centerline of the base board. Now turn the board over and drill a 5/8" hole just deep enough to contain the head of the carriage bolt at each guide hole. Turn the board over again and drill a 5/16" hole for the carriage bolt. Test fit the sliding fence with the bolts in place to see if it moves without binding.

10. Apply an Oil Finish

Wipe on three or four coats of oil and allow to thoroughly dry (at least 48 hours) before permanently attaching the sliding stop — otherwise the oil between the boards will take forever to dry.

Workbench Tote

THE PROJECT:

I like to work with an uncluttered bench, but I don't like drawers on my bench because they regularly get in the way of bench dogs and clamps and add a step to gaining access to a tool (Like the pre-industrial artisans, I like open shelves and hooks). So to keep various bench paraphernalia from getting scattered and lost in shavings I designed this small tote to contain them. It usually sits readily accessible either on the bench's lower shelf — or sometimes on the bench itself. In it I keep items such as small layout tools; wood clamping pads and wedges; scraps of leather; and a brass, plane-blade adjusting hammer. This tote is an excellent first, all-handtool furniture(ish) project that will put many of the fixtures you've built (and the skills you've gained) to work while introducing a few new ones!

The tote features simple lap joints at the corners (nailed with decorative, rose-headed copper nails) and a handle/divider set into stopped da-does in the end pieces. This simple joint gives the divider ample strength to act as a handle to pick up the tote without needing additional fasteners such as screws, nails or even glue for strength. The bottom of the tote is a thin piece of wood beveled at the edges to fit into a groove plowed into the four sides.

In this final project you'll get to put into practice methods of design and layout based on classic orders of proportion and geometry. Instead of working to measurements, you will lay out the length of the parts by proportioning them in whole numbers to the width of the stock you want to use to make the sidewalls of the tote. As you can see in the drawing, that means the length of the end pieces is simply three times their width (a 1:3 ratio) and the length of the sides is twice the length of the end (1:2). At its apex, the height of the handle is twice the height of the sides (measured from the top edge to the groove). To my eye, this simple proportioning scheme results in a very pleasing and functional shape for this tote.

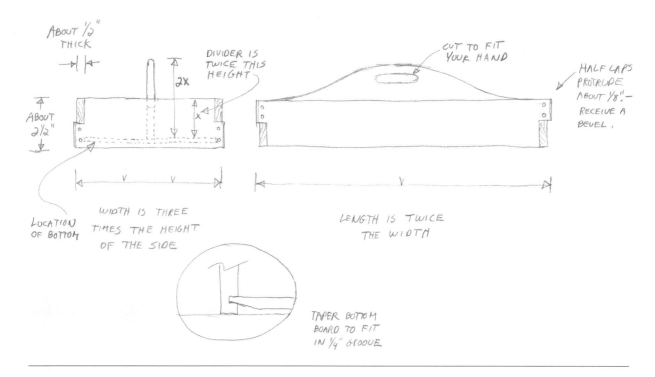

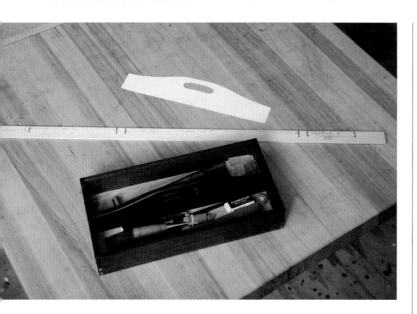

No drawings, no numbers: All the information needed to build this bench tote is permanently recorded on a stick and a scrap of posterboard. The latter represents the curved top edge and handle hole of the tote's divider, while the former has tick marks that represent the length and width of the sides and ends as well as the size and location of the various joints.

THE PROCESS:

1. Select the Stock

Since this project is the first furniture-like project we'll do in this book, I suggest that you pick out a board of nicely figured, handtool-friendly domestic hardwood such as cherry or walnut. If you can get the board already planed to ½" thick, then so much the better. Many hardwood lumber yards carry ½" stock in hardwood to satisfy the demand of commercial cabinetshops for solid-wood drawer stock. If, however, you have to start with ¾" stock, surface plane it equally from both faces (by hand or by machine) to minimize the board's potential for distortion or resaw it from a piece of 4/4 stock. Another option is to start with 5/4 stock and resaw it in half. If you go this route, you can layout the sides and ends to create a continuous grain pattern around the circumference of the tote. The drawing at right illustrates this process.

SKILLS INTRODUCED:

Designing to whole-number proportions; making up and laying out with "tick" sticks and dividers; making a stopped dado; using the sticking board to hold stock for plowing; beveling a field to fit a groove; and making lap joints (precision sawing and paring to a chisel guide).

TOOLS INTRODUCED:

Use of sector; use of sticking board; dovetail saw.

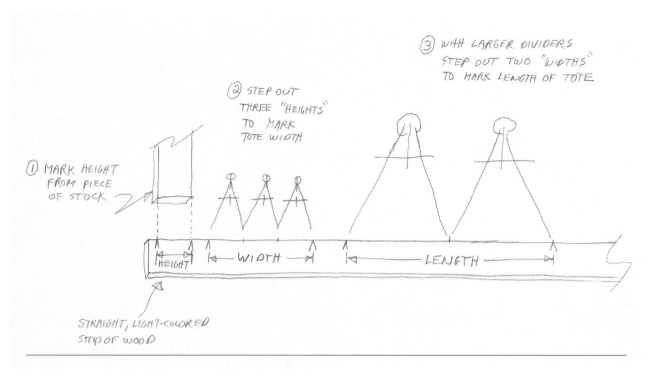

③ WITH LARGER DIVIDERS STEP OUT TWO "WIDTHS" TO MARK LENGTH OF TOTE

② STEP OUT THREE "HEIGHTS" TO MARK TOTE WIDTH

① MARK HEIGHT FROM PIECE OF STOCK

HEIGHT   WIDTH   LENGTH

STRAIGHT, LIGHT-COLORED STRIP OF WOOD

DEVELOPMENT OF TICK STICK

① SELECT STOCK ABOUT ¼" THICKER THAN TWICE THE FINISHED THICKNESS OF COMPONENTS

② LAYOUT COMPONENTS FROM TICK STICK ON FACES AS SHOWN. MARK OUT SIDE FACE.

③ RESAW DOWN MIDDLE

④ PLANE SMOOTH

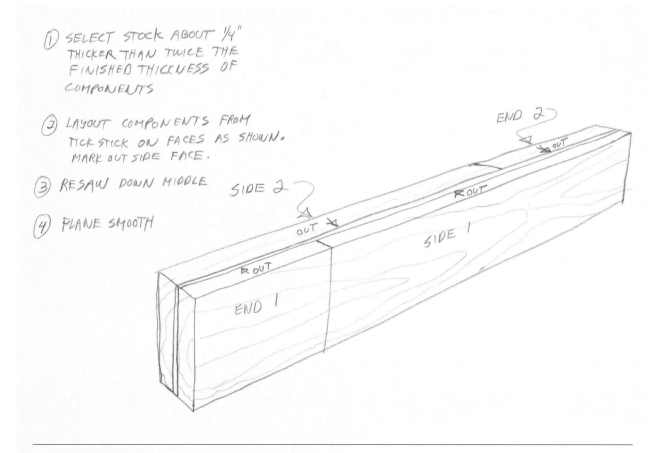

END 2

OUT

SIDE 2

OUT

OUT

SIDE 1

OUT

END 1

LAYOUT OF BOX COMPONENTS FOR CONTIGUOUS GRAIN ON A LENGTH OF RESAWN STOCK

Here I'm using the "tick stick" to lay out the sides and ends of the tote on a length of stock.

The two lengths of stock that will each become a side and an end of the tote need to be made exactly the same height. To quickly accomplish that, I insert both of them into the edge planing stop and trim both edges at the same time with my fore plane.

2. Size the Stock to Width and Rough Length

Begin the layout process by creating a tick stick that will represent the length of the various parts of the tote, including the divider and its tenons. The drawing at the top of page 149 illustrates how to develop the lengths of the parts using a pair of dividers. You don't necessarily need to make a full-scale drawing except for laying out the curve of the top edge of the dividers. After ripping out stock to width, lay the tick stick on the stock to mark out the length of the various parts, including the divider and the bottom panel. You will cut all these parts oversize so they can be fitted and trimmed precisely to match and to fit one another.

For ease of handling the stock on the sticking board when plowing the groove for the bottom panel, I recommend that you cut out two pieces just long enough to produce a side and an end. To ensure these pieces are exactly the same width, true one edge of each board and then set both of them into the edge-planing stop, trued edge down. Then gang-plane the top edge. Remove them from this fixture and set up the face- planing stop. Use your smoothing plane to remove any mill marks and to mirror-smooth the faces of these two pieces as well as the divider and bottom panel.

3. Plow the Grooves for the Bottom Board

Use your plow plane to create a ¼"-wide groove along the inside of the ends and sides about ³⁄₁₆" in from the bottom edge. Set one of the boards

To ensure a perfectly true starting point, I use my bench hook as a shooting board to guide my low-angle jack plane across the end of the stock. Note how the second hook supports the overhang.

After laying out a cut with my try square and marking knife, I use the bench hook to support the stock as I cut it to length with a crosscut-filed backsaw.

To ensure the second side component is exactly the same length as the first, I use the latter as a layout template. I use a marking knife — which creates a much more precise line than a pencil — to mark the cutline.

in your sticking board so that its edge overhangs the fixture's base, allowing the edge of the stock to serve as a guide for the side fence of the plow plane. (If you haven't built your sticking board yet, you can clamp the stock in a tail vise so that its edge overhangs the edge of the bench or you can raise it up on an underlying board to expose the reference edge.) If the boards have any bow to them, place them convex face up to ensure you plow the groove to its full depth along the full length of the board. Create a tool track for the plow plane blade as described in the last project by making a series of short, over-lapping strokes working from the far to the near end and then plow the depth of the groove in a series of passes to you arrive at one-third the thickness of the stock.

4. Lay Out and Cut the Parts to Finished Length

True the end of the stock using your bench hook as a shooting board, and then lay out one of the sidepieces from your tick stick. Saw and true this component, then use it as a template to precisely lay out its matching sidepiece. Repeat this procedure for the end pieces.

5. Lay Out the Stopped Dadoes for the Divider

Select one of your bench chisels whose width is slightly less than the thickness of the stock for the divider. Find the center of the end pieces by stepping over with dividers and then prick a centerline mark. Center your chisel on the mark

Using a wide chisel, I chop down along the knifed registration lines to make the side walls of the stopped dado. I work in stages chopping and then paring to create a V until I reach the bottom of the dado. A piece of tape on the chisel acts as a visual depth mark.

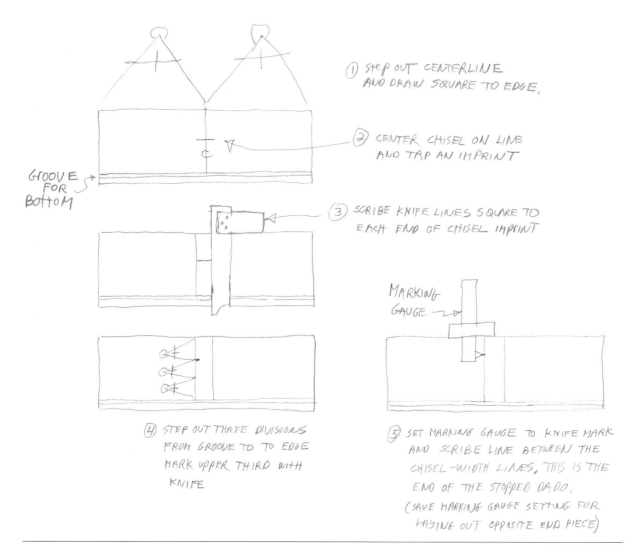

① STEP OUT CENTERLINE AND DRAW SQUARE TO EDGE.

② CENTER CHISEL ON LINE AND TAP AN IMPRINT

GROOVE FOR BOTTOM

③ SCRIBE KNIFE LINES SQUARE TO EACH END OF CHISEL IMPRINT

MARKING GAUGE

④ STEP OUT THREE DIVISIONS FROM GROOVE TO TO EDGE MARK UPPER THIRD WITH KNIFE

⑤ SET MARKING GAUGE TO KNIFE MARK AND SCRIBE LINE BETWEEN THE CHISEL-WIDTH LINES, THIS IS THE END OF THE STOPPED DADO. (SAVE MARKING GAUGE SETTING FOR LAYING OUT OPPOSITE END PIECE)

DETAIL: LAYOUT OF STOPPED DADO ON BENCH TOTE

After making the side walls, I clean out the waste between by paring in from the end of the stopped dado with a paring chisel. I begin by angling the chisel toward each wall creating a "mountain" of waste between.

(your eyeball guess is plenty accurate enough) and tap it to impress a width mark. Lay out the cutlines of the dado at each end of the width mark using a square and a marking knife.

To mark the extent of the stopped dado, use your dividers to step out the width of the end piece above the groove in thirds, then set your marking gauge to the upper third mark and scribe the stop line for the dado. Lay out the second end piece, using the first end piece as a guide for transferring the measurements with a pair of dividers.

6. Cut Out the Dado

Using your sharp layout knife, deepen the dado layout lines and make a registration "wall" by cutting in at an angle from the waste side of the lines. Now deepen the lines further using a wide chisel (wide enough so it takes only three steps to cover the extent of the stopped dado). Indicate the depth of the dado on the face of the chisel with a piece of tape. Tap down in one-eighth inch deep increments along the length of the dado on each side, then remove the waste to create a deep "V." The registration wall you created earlier will prevent the chisel from widening the dado past the layout line.

When you've chopped down to the full depth of the dado (which will be equal to the depth of the plowed groove for the bottom panel), clean out the waste with your first chisel (sized to the width of the dado), by coming into the dado from the bottom edge of the endpiece, first tilt-

ing the chisel to one side, then the other. There will be a "V"-shaped mountain of waste in the middle that you will remove by holding the chisel flat to the bottom of the dado. If you have a small router plane, use it for the last few strokes to clean up and precisely level the bottom of the dado.

7. Layout and Cut the Lap Joints
Mark the depth of the laps by setting the marking gauge to the thickness of the stock and then add ⅛" for the decorative protrusion. Scribe the line around the end of each side and endpiece. Next, find the centerpoint of the two laps by stepping in from each end with your dividers.

Here I'm holding the chisel flat to pare away the top of the "mountain."

I follow up the chisel with a small router plane to make the bottom of the dado smooth and to the precise depth.

After sawing the lap joints, I set up a block in the end vise to guide my paring chisel to quickly and precisely trim the joint to the scribed layout lines. Here I'm lightly tapping the stock with the handle of my chisel to align it precisely with the top edge of the guide block.

I use my thumb to hold the back of the chisel to the top of the block as I pare away the waste down to the joint's scribe lines.

Set the marking gauge to this mark and mark the ends of each board to delineate the two lap joints. Clearly mark the waste areas with a China wax pencil.

Using your dovetail saw, saw to the waste side of the centerline and then crosscut off the waste, leaving about 1/32" of extra material in the end grain waste area for final trimming with a paring chisel. Set up the pieces in a vise with the chisel guide set precisely to the scribed layout line. Select a very sharp chisel (wider than the stock) and pare to the line by pressing the back of the chisel on the guide block. Use a shearing action to ease the cut. (This is why paring chisels have longer handles — to provide leverage for this purpose.) If you encounter too much back pressure trying to do it in one pass, take the waste off in steps until you reach the guide block.

Using your trimming plane, create a small bevel around the end of each lap. These bevels will protrude past the sides and ends, visually accentuating the joint (and helping to hide any gaps).

8. Shape the Divider

Lay out the curved top edge of the divider using a thin batten or a selection of French curves. When the curve looks good to your eye, it is good! Cut to the curved line with a bow or coping saw and then clean up the saw cut with a spokeshave.

Next, lay out the cutout for the handle as specified in the drawing. As you have done earlier when making the handle for the straightedge, drill out a hole at each end of the layout with a brace and centerpoint bit, being very careful not to drill all the way through from one side. Use a keyhole saw to cut out the waste between the holes. Clean up the saw cut and bevel around the edges of the handle hole with a small cabinetmaker's half-round rasp followed by a half-round file. Alternatively, you can stick sandpaper to a dowel to substitute for a file.

9. Cut the Divider to Length

To cut the divider board to the exact length needed to span between the bottoms of the

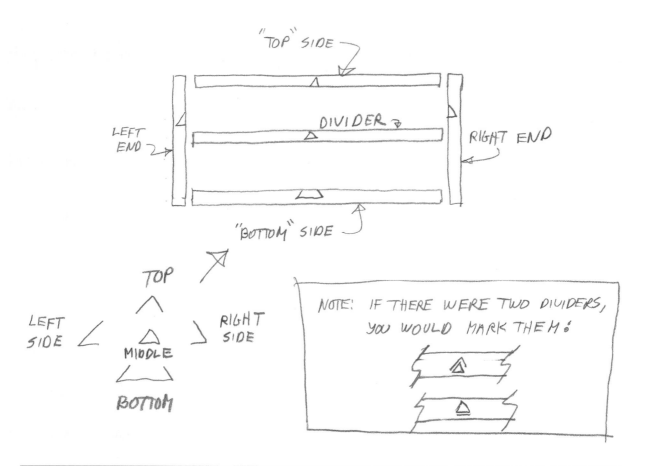

PYRAMID SYMBOL MARKING SYSTEM

To ensure that the divider is exactly the right length to fill the dados at each end of the tote, I lay out its length directly to the dry-assembled ends and sides. My end vise acts as a clamp to hold the assembly temporarily together.

dados in the endpieces, dry-assemble the end and side pieces upside-down and hold and mark the divider directly to the bottom of the dados. Be sure to center the piece first. Now mark all the pieces with pyramid symbols to keep them oriented to one another throughout the rest of the process. Cut the divider to length.

10. Fit the Divider

Lay out the tenon (the portion of the stock that will fit into the dado) as shown on page 156. Cut the tenons to length with a back saw and then scribe one side to the depth of the dado. Use a small shoulder plane to remove waste until the tenon fits snugly in the dado. You shouldn't need a fence or guide for this small adjustment — just freehand the tool to the scribe line.

RIGHT Because I made the dado slightly thinner than the divider, I trim the side of the stub tenon on the divider with a small shoulder plane to create a gap-free fit.

Here I'm directly marking the length of the stub tenon on the end of the divider that will fit the stopped dado.

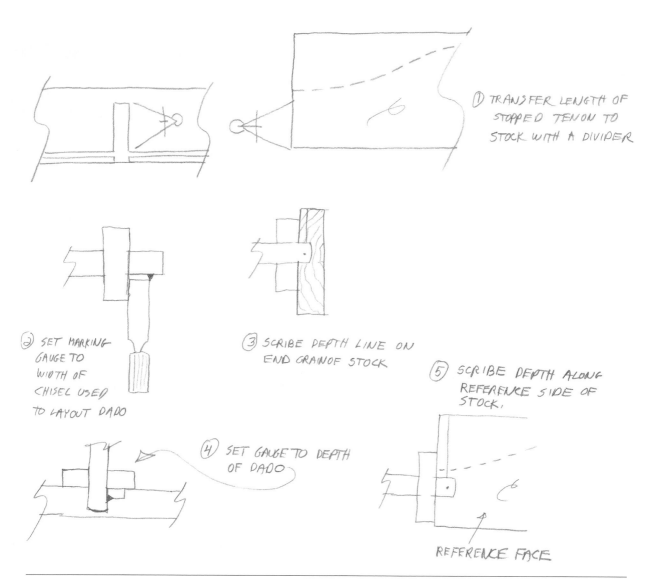

① TRANSFER LENGTH OF STOPPED TENON TO STOCK WITH A DIVIDER

② SET MARKING GAUGE TO WIDTH OF CHISEL USED TO LAYOUT DADO

③ SCRIBE DEPTH LINE ON END GRAIN OF STOCK

④ SET GAUGE TO DEPTH OF DADO

⑤ SCRIBE DEPTH ALONG REFERENCE SIDE OF STOCK,

REFERENCE FACE

DETAIL OF DIVIDER TENON LAYOUT TO STOPPED DADO

Here I'm using the divider to directly lay out the length of the bottom panel (because the grooves for the panel are the same depth as the dado for the divider).

11. Make the Bottom Panel

Lay out the width of the bottom panel directly from the dry assembly and the panel's length from the divider. Subtract about ⅛" from the width (to allow for wood movement), but make the length just a hair shy to ensure the joints close tightly. (The panel won't expand along its grain). Cut the bottom panel to size with a panel saw (it doesn't need to be rip-filed for this thin stock), trim planing to size as necessary.

Use your block plane or a small bench plane (I can handle a #3 in one hand) to taper a field around the perimeter of the bottom panel to fit into the plowed groove. The panel is small and light enough to secure by hand in your bench hook. Test the fit in one of the side pieces.

Using a wax pencil and my fingers as a marking gauge, I lay out the extent of the taper that I'll make on the bottom of the bottom panel to fit its edges into the plowed groove.

With the panel held tight to the bench hook's back stop, I single-hand my freshly sharpened #3 bench plane to quickly waste away the taper.

12. Assemble the Tote

Insert the divider into the stopped dados at each end piece and then slide in the bottom panel. Set the assembly on its side and install the first sidepiece after spreading a thin film of glue on the mating surfaces. Install the second sidepiece and then clamp the pieces just firmly enough to fully seat all the joints. Use your try square to check that the assembly is square. Wait for the glue to dry and then lay out the nail holes with a pair of dividers. Pre-drill for the copper nails and then tap them in gently with a plastic-headed hammer.

ABOVE RIGHT With the parts set on leveled supports on my assembly table, I insert the divider into its stopped tenons and then capture the bottom panel between the end boards.

BOTTOM RIGHT I apply a thin film of glue to the meeting surfaces of the lap joints and then clamp the assembly together. The glue will seal the end grain and help hold everything together while I drill for, and install, the copper nails.

To make the plugs that will fill — and completely hide — the exposed bottom panel grooves I set a scrap upright in my vise and saw out slightly tapered wedges.

Here I'm inserting the wedges into the exposed grooves with my wood-tipped brass mallet. A thin film of glue will hold them in place. Later, I'll saw and trim them flush.

The wedge in place

The wedge is cut flush, no way can you see where it is!

13. Fill the Exposed Grooves

While we could have avoided having exposed bottom panel grooves by second-lapping the bottom lap joint, the complication wouldn't have been worth the effort. You would have ended up with the visual distraction of two different-sized lap joints! Instead, we can solve the problem by simply filling the gap with a wedge of the same material as the lap joint.

Use a piece of scrap taken from the same material you made the side pieces from to cut out some wedge-shaped pieces whose mid-area is the same size in cross section as the groove. Apply a thin film of glue and tap them in place. When dry, cut and pare them flush.

14. Apply a Finish

Finally: A reason to apply oil that isn't primarily for the purpose of stabilizing the wood. Instead, the oil will also enhance the color and grain of the wood and make this tote just beautiful! On my tote, I applied a coat of oil (for color) followed by about six coats of shellac.

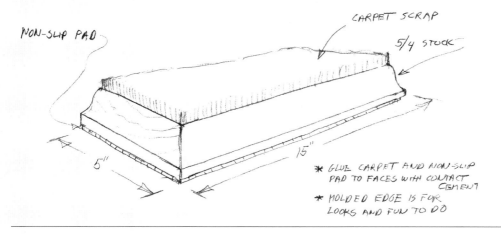

NON-SLIP PAD

CARPET SCRAP

5/4 STOCK

15"

5"

* GLUE CARPET AND NON-SLIP PAD TO FACES WITH CONTACT CEMENT
* MOLDED EDGE IS FOR LOOKS AND FUN TO DO

OILING PAD

Oiling Pad

For all the advantages of the steel-bodied plane over the traditional wood planes, it does have one (some would say there are more) inherent disadvantage: steel tends to stick to wood. There is a lot less friction to overcome when you rub wood over wood. The treatment for this problem is to keep the sole of your steel plane constantly lubricated while you use it, even if you have applied paste wax. This oiling pad fixture, sitting on your workbench, makes it easy, fast and convenient to wipe on a thin coat of oil (usually camillia or another plant-based, non-drying oil). Everytime you swipe your plane across the pad, the decrease in back pressure will make you feel as if you have just sharpened your plane.

CONSTRUCTION:
Find a piece of scrap 5/4 stock about a half-a-foot by a foot-and-a-half; work a nice decorative profile around its edge (for show and fun); use contact cement to attache a scrap of carpet to the top, and a piece of non-skid drawer liner to the bottom and you're done!

USE:
I keep the pad sitting on my planing bench parallel to, and just to the side of, where I plane boards secured in my tail vise. As I plane, I occasionally draw the plane backward across the carpet and continue working almost uninterrupted. For maintenance, I regularly brush shavings out of the carpet and squirt a bit of oil along its length.

Diagonal Testing Stick

This lay-out tool offers you a quick and accurate way to test and to set a rectilinear construction perfectly square without having to resort to taking measurements or using a square (which can be inaccurate if the sides of the structure aren't perfectly straight).

CONSTRUCTION:
Make the stick from 4/4 stock of any wood as long as its relatively straight-grained. The length can be anywhere from 2- to 4-ft. or more, though I find 3-ft. serves to measure most drawers and smaller furniture pieces. While you don't have to taper the stick, it is a good planing exercise and it makes the stick a bit lighter and easier to manipulate — and it looks like a tool, not just a stick with a pointy end! Note that the point of the stick must be at an acute angle to allow it to

swivel in the corner of a rectangle without hitting the sidewall. Conversely, the inner notch (see the illustraion at right), must be an obtuse angle for the same reason.

USE:
• Step 1: Set the stick into one corner of the box (or if you don't have access to the inside corner, set the inner notch over the outside corner) and make a mark on the stick at the opposite corner. I put on a strip of masking tape in the area to be marked to make the mark clearer and to make it instantly erasable.

• Step 2: Set the stick at the adjacent corner and mark the stick again at the opposite corner.

• Step 3: If both marks are at exactly the same place, the structure is exactly square. If not, make a mark between them on center and shift the structure so the corner comes to this centerline mark.

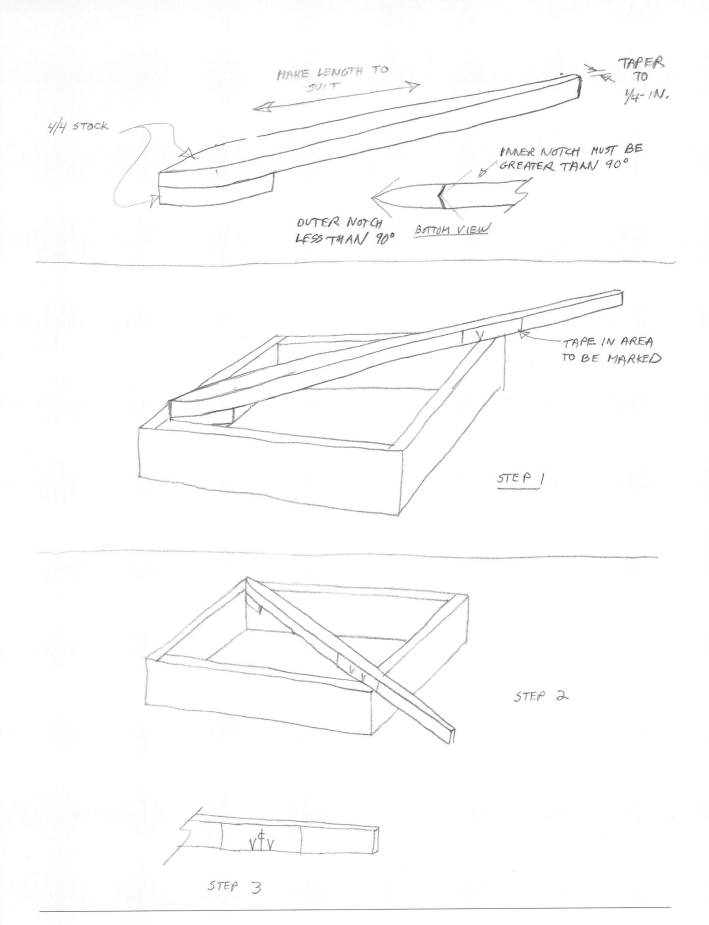

MAKE LENGTH TO SUIT

TAPER TO ¼-IN.

4/4 STOCK

INNER NOTCH MUST BE GREATER THAN 90°

OUTER NOTCH LESS THAN 90°

BOTTOM VIEW

TAPE IN AREA TO BE MARKED

STEP 1

STEP 2

STEP 3

DIAGONAL TESTING STICK

Vise for Sharpening Saws and Scrapers

This simple wooden-jaw vise holds small saw and scraper blades securely and sets up quickly in most types of woodworking vises. I use it mostly in the double screw vise at my joinery bench, as that brings it to a comfortable working height for me. I veneer the top jaws with a thin strip of leather or rubber (as from a bicycle tire tube) to help hold the blades without slipping and to dampen the vibration of filing.

CONSTRUCTION:

I made my vise from ¾"-thick scraps of poplar and cherry pulled from my waste bin. The dimensions aren't particular crucial — the only critical dimension to watch out for is to size the pair of jaws at the top (including the leather or rubber veneer) to come out just a hair narrower than the 1"-width of the bottom spacer. This allows the vise to stand open slightly, allowing you to easily insert a saw or scraper blade.

Cut all the parts to size, then nail or screw the top jaws to the inside top of the sides and apply the leather or rubber veneer. Next rabbet the side ledgers as shown and then screw them in place. Finally, screw both sides to the bottom spacer.

USE:

To use the vise, drop it into a bench-mounted vise so that its jaws engage the rabbets of the ledger strips (see the end view detail). Slide in the blade to be sharpened and tighten down the bench vise with just enough force to keep the blade from slipping. Don't over-crank the vise or you may crush this fixture!

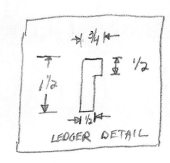

3/4

1/2

1 1/2

1/2

LEDGER DETAIL

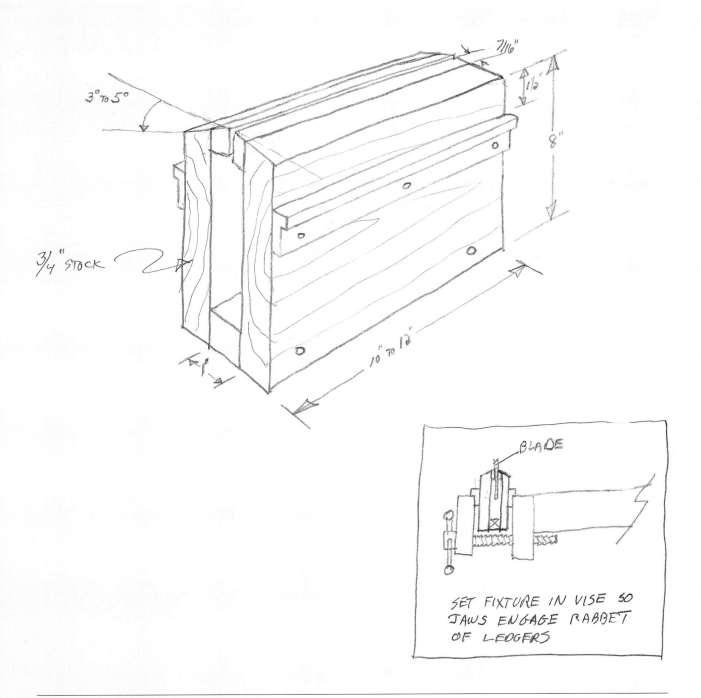

7/16"

3° to 5°

1 1/2"

8"

3/4" STOCK

10" to 12"

1"

BLADE

SET FIXTURE IN VISE SO
JAWS ENGAGE RABBET
OF LEDGERS

VISE FOR SMALL BACKSAWS AND SCRAPER BLADES

Sawbench Pair

When you use a full-size hand saw to crosscut a board to length or to rip it to width, about the only way you will make full use of the length of the saw's blade (which speeds up the cut and helps keep the saw sharper for longer) is to position the board at the right height to take full advantage of the pumping action of your sawing arm. For most people, this height falls at about the top of their knee cap — and this is the height I recommend that you should build your saw bench. Additional features that make a sawbench as efficient as possible are: A stable and secure footprint; a wide top surface; and a provision for holddowns. I have also designed the benches to work together to hold a board for ripping without presenting any obstructions to the saw and without having to shift the board — significant time savers.

CONSTRUCTION:
I built my benches from construction grade lumber: 2×4's and 2×6's. I was being cheap — you could select some nice hardwood (such as ash) to make them a bit more presentable as well as a bit heavier — and therefore even more stable.

Lay out the end view of the bench, full scale, on a large sheet of paper so you can directly measure the angles and lengths of the legs. To add strength, notch the legs around the top board rather than just pegging or lag-bolting them in place. You can also notch the top board to capture the sides of the legs. To ensure dimensional stability, lap the lower rail and lap the end gussets over the legs. After you have assembled the benches, set them on a flat surface (here's where that assembly table comes in handy) and then trim the bottom of the legs so the bench top is level and the assembly doesn't rock.

USE:
For crosscutting, I orient the benches so that the plumb side of the bench faces outward and toward the ends of the workpiece to be cut. This keeps the legs out of the way of the crosscutting action. With larger boards, I often tap at least one of the holddowns over the board to prevent it from shifting.

For ripping, I draw the benches together, plumb sides facing one another and spaced a couple of inches apart. I orient the workpiece so that the cut line falls over the gap and then secure it in place along one side with the two holddowns.

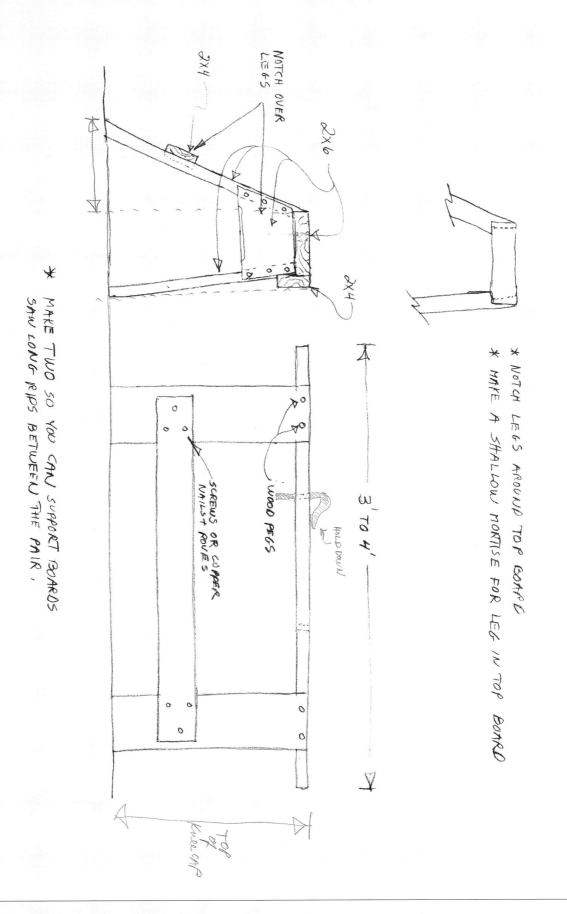

NOTCH OVER LEGS

2x4

2x6

NOTCH OVER LEGS

2x4

* MAKE TWO SO YOU CAN SUPPORT BOARDS SAW LONG RIPS BETWEEN THE PAIR.

SCREWS OR COPPER NAILS + ROVES

WOOD PEGS

HOLD DOWN

3' TO 4'

TOP OF KNEE CAP

* NOTCH LEGS AROUND TOP BOARD
* MAKE A SHALLOW MORTISE FOR LEG IN TOP BOARD

SAWBENCH

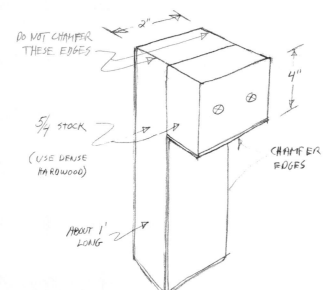

DO NOT CHAMFER
THESE EDGES

2"

4"

5/4 STOCK

(USE DENSE
HARDWOOD)

CHAMFER
EDGES

ABOUT 1'
LONG

WASTE BACKING BLOCK

* GLUE AND SCREW
PARTS TOGETHER

* DO NOT CHAMFER
AROUND TOP OF
BLOCK

Waste Backing Block

One of the most common problems encountered when planing end grain is tearout on the far side of the stroke. While you can avoid this by planing in from each end, or — if you have good hand-eye coordination — rotating the plane to 90 degrees to the direction of travel at the end of the stroke. The most foolproof technique is to back up the workpiece with another board. This fixture is that board — but designed to support itself as you capture it in the vise behind your workpiece.

CONSTRUCTION:
For longevity, I make my fixture from some 5/4 hard-maple scrap. Any other dense hardwood would serve as well. I chamfer all the edges except the two upper edges as shown (so they can bear against the workpiece without a gap), and then glue and screw the two components together.

USE:
Open up your vise (usually the tail vise) to accept the workpiece, plus the fixture. Drop the fixture in place and then insert the workpiece so that its top edge is aligned even with the top of the fixture. Lock them together in the vise and then plane away at the end grain toward the fixture.

Drawing Bows

There are many occasions in the design of a furniture piece where you have need of drawing an arc of a circle — or the constantly changing radius of a French curve. You can use a large compass or a set of trammel points for the former, and a set of ship curves for the latter. Or you can make up these simple tools to accomplish the same thing with a lot less hassle. Depending on how long you make the sticks, you can create any size or radius curve you wish.

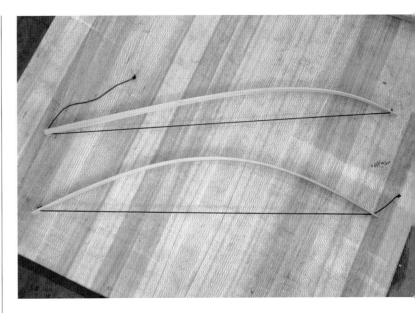

CONSTRUCTION:

To insure that the bows will make fair curves, be careful to select the straightest grain wood you can find. Ideally, you want nearly all the grain lines to run from one end to the other, both on the face and on the edge of the stick. If you don't find a stick that meets these criteria in your scrap bin, lay out the cut parallel to the grain on a piece of stock and cut it out. It doesn't matter, by the way, how you orient the grain on the face (the wider part) of the sticks — in my experience, either orientation will produce fair curves. Before cutting a slot in the ends of the stick to receive the string, drill a hole at the end point of the cut — this will prevent splitting. I file the slot into a wedge shape so I can simply jam the string

in the slot at the desired setting. Install a string by making a figure eight knot at one end and feed the string into the hole at one end. The knot will prevent the string from pulling through. Leave the other end loose.

USE

To set the desired curve, simply bend the bow and then secure it to that shape by jamming the loose end of the string into the slot at the opposite end of the stick.

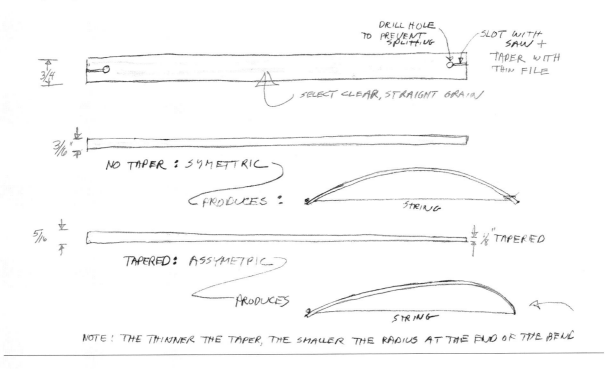

DRILL HOLE TO PREVENT SPLITTING

SLOT WITH SAW + TAPER WITH THIN FILE

3/4"

SELECT CLEAR, STRAIGHT GRAIN

3/16"

NO TAPER : SYMETTRIC — PRODUCES :

STRING

5/16"

1/8" TAPERED

TAPERED : ASSYMETRIC — PRODUCES

STRING

NOTE : THE THINNER THE TAPER, THE SMALLER THE RADIUS AT THE END OF THE BEND

Sticking Board for Dowels

To meet the challenge of securing small pieces of a stock for planing, especially when creating round dowels from square stock, you need a "sticking board" to hold the workpiece. This version, made from a length of 5/4 stock, is modified with a groove so you can set the square stock with its corners oriented vertically.

CONSTRUCTION:
Select a piece of straight 5/4 stock about 2' long and plow a ¼"-wide groove about ¼" deep along one edge. Set a flat head screw into the groove at one end — this will bear against the end of the workpiece and can be adjusted in height as necessary.

USE:
Set the fixture into a vise or capture it between bench dogs, and then set your workpiece (a stick sized square to the desired width of the finished dowel) into the grove with one corner facing up with the end bearing against the screw. Plane a facet on this corner, counting the full-length strokes. Stop after four to six strokes and turn the workpiece to plane the opposite corner the same number of strokes. Repeat on the two remaining corners and check to see if all the facets are of even width. Add strokes to the corner facets, a

stroke or two at a time, until they are. The stick will now be a hexagon, and that is usually good enough for use as a peg in a joint. If you want it round, plane facets on the eight corners and then sand the dowel perfectly round.

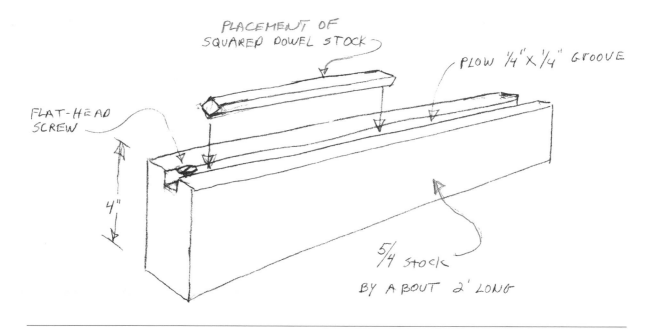

PLACEMENT OF SQUARED DOWEL STOCK

PLOW ¼" X ¼" GROOVE

FLAT-HEAD SCREW

4"

5/4 STOCK

BY ABOUT 2' LONG

STICKING BOARD FOR DOWELS

Six Square Process

TO MAKE A BOARD TRUE ON ALL
ITS FACES AND EDGES FOLLOW
THESE STEPS:

1. Cut the board to rough length with a cross-cut handsaw.

2. Lay the board on your (trued-flat) bench-top and see if it rocks. Try both sides. If it rocks lengthwise, the board has a bow. If it rocks side to side, it has a cup. Mark the high spots on the concave side. If, however, the board rocks corner to corner, it's warped, and in this case mark the high corners. If any of these conditions are severe — say more than 1/8", I recommend you find another board — I'm convinced that pre-industrial artisans were that picky as well!

3. Secure the board on the bench between two bench dogs, with the high spots on the edges or ends facing up. If the board rocks (which it likely will), insert some shims to stabilize it. It must not move under the force of planing!

4. Use a scrub plane or a jack plane with a strongly-cambered blade (8" to 10" radius) to remove the high spots. Work directly across the grain and take the thickest shavings you can reasonably push through the plane. Concentrate

Testing face of board for flat by pressing down onto benchtop.

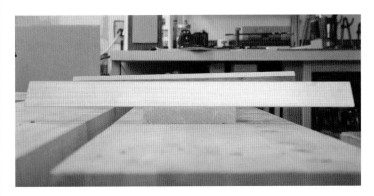

Testing face for twist with winding sticks, from the woodworker's point of view. High spots on the board are marked with a China pencil.

Testing face with a straight edge. Where light is visible through gaps, the board face is not flat.

Scrub planing directly across board — high spots are marked on the face.

Planing the face at a diagonal with a jackplane.

first on the high spots at the ends or edges, but be careful not to overdo it and create low spots! Continue until your straight edge indicates that the high spots have been leveled (no gap under the edge anywhere). Use your winding sticks to check to see if the twist is gone.

5. When the bow, cup or twist is largely corrected (on the face you are working on), back off the blade and push the plane diagonally across the board, working from one end to the other. You may find that one direction works easier than the other because of the board's inherent grain direction. You should be able to produce a continuous shaving from one edge to the other. To better see your progress, make a crosshatching of lines with your China pencil perpendicular to the run of the plane. Be careful not to take more strokes at the ends of the board than you take in between — otherwise you will introduce (or reintroduce) a convex curve along the length of the board.

6. If you find that you have the tendency to reintroduce twist by planing from only one edge of the board, flip it end for end (redo your shims to keep the board stable), and diagonally plane from the other edge, working from one end to the other.

Planing face at diagonal in the other direction, with the board flipped end for end.

7. Now switch to a try plane. Set it for a medium-coarse shaving (about .005" thick) and run it from one end to the other. Take overlapping strokes, sort of like mowing a lawn. At first only the tops of the diagonal grooves will come off, then full shavings. To ease the backpressure, back off on the thickness of the shavings. Be very careful to keep a lot of pressure, however, on the sole ahead of the blade when starting the cut, and shift the pressure to the rear of the plane as you approach the far end. Use your straightedge to check to be sure you aren't planing in a long concave bow — which is, you'll discover, our natural tendency if we get sloppy with our handling of the plane. Also, avoid double planing at each edge. This will introduce a convex curve across the width of the board.

8. When you are satisfied that this face is flat, you now have a true reference face.

9. The next step is to create a true edge on one side of the board. Use your try plane to make it straight along its length and perpendicular to the face you just flattened.

10. Now use a panel gauge or a combination square and pencil and mark out the desired width of the board from the trued edge. Rip (or scrub plane down to) the cutline and then true this edge. Mark it with a squiggle to indicate its also been trued.

11. Next, create a parallel reference face on the opposite side of the board. Start by setting your marking gauge to the thickness that you

Planing the face lengthwise with a try plane.

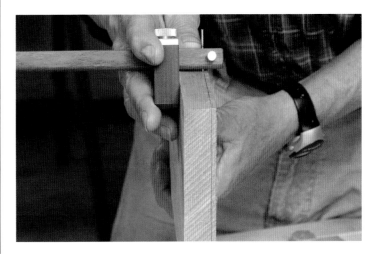

Marking the board's final thickness with a panel gauge.

Plane a bevel all around the circumference of the board to the thickness of the scribe line.

Marking china lines across the bevels.

wish the board to be. Unclamp the board and scribe this line on all the edges and darken the line with a pencil. If the edges are rough, you may need to plane the roughness off first — but don't worry about making these edges true yet.

12. Plane a bevel on the non-reference face of the board around its circumference with your aggressive jack plane, bringing the bottom edge of the bevel just to the scribe line. This bevel will give you a clear visual reference to where you are in the surface planing process and, as the bevel gets smaller, will warn you when you are getting close to the scribe line. Using your China pencil, make lines across the bevel so you can clearly track your progress as you approach the hard-to-see layout lines on the edges of the board.

13. Repeat the planing process in steps 5 through 7 above until you are satisfied that the second face is flat and parallel to the first reference face.

Checking the edge for square (above). Changing the angle of edge by holding the side of sole even with corner (right).

14. Using a jack-sized block plane with a freshly sharpened blade, true one end of the board square to the face and square to the side edge (again, the square should read true from either side edge if they are parallel (i.e. true to one another). To prevent splitting out at the exit edge of the plane stroke, back up the edge with a scrap board as shown in the middle, left photo. If you would like an excuse to buy and use another type of plane, you can use an edge trimming plane (freshly sharpened!) to make the final few strokes across the end of the board, ensuring a perfect 90° angle. Mark a squiggle on this end.

15. Finally, measure over from the trued end and mark the desired length of the board. To prevent tear-out, scribe the line all the way around the board with a marking knife, then saw to the line. Follow with the block plane to create the last, sixth, true surface on the board.

16. To test the board for true, hold a square along one edge and mark a line across the face with a fine pencil. Square this line across the far edge and then draw the line square across the other face. Now square up from this line. If the edges were straight and parallel the line should meet the starting point of the first line. Repeat this test working from the end of the board.

17. If the test lines are positive, you're done. With practice, you will have come to this point (say on a drawer-faced sized board) in about the same time it took me to write this process down!

Truing the edge, showing proper hand positiong.

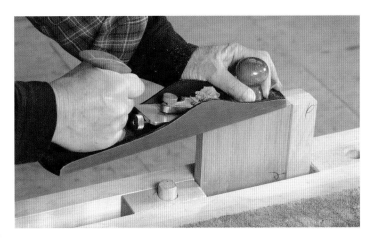

Truing end with jack-size block plane, backup block in place (above). Truing end with edge-trimming plane (below).

CLOSING THOUGHTS....

As I write this epilogue its been over a year since I began writing this book. It's also been that long since I gave the last of my hand power tools (and most of my stationary machines) to a young man in my family who is setting up to work wood for a living. So now comes the moment of truth: What has it really been like for me — a production tradesman for three decades — to shift to working wood for fun using hand tools almost exclusively?

Well, to be honest, it hasn't always been fun and it hasn't always been easy. Taking the time to properly set up and sharpen the tools to their peak potential wasn't the hard part. That part was fun, in fact, and it really didn't take all that long. Getting my muscles and endurance up to speed for the increased physical demands of working these tools with only the power of my body was a bit less fun. (Though I'm told exercise is good for me at my age!) What was hard for me, however, was adjusting myself to the mindset and work pace of the pre-industrial, hand-tool artisan. It took me almost a full year to finally stop seeing the product done and to simply immerse myself in the process — the simple joy of working the wood with sharp tools and the power of my hands and body.

Since that shift took place I now find myself actually looking forward to planing, to cutting joints, to crosscutting and to ripping (admittedly in small doses!) stock by hand. As I continue to build furniture primarily with hand tools in my basement workshop, my initial reasons and hopes for making this transformation have been born out:

- Unlike my power tool days, I can now go down to the shop and work any time, day or night, without any worry about disturbing my family. They can even be in the shop with me doing other projects … because there is no longer any reason they can't.
- I get to work in a clean shop — there is no longer a coating of dust everywhere.
- I'm actually getting to talk with friends as they come by — without stopping working. I'm even thinking of putting in an easy chair for them!
- I now know what the lyrics are to the songs on many of my old CDs — because I can now hear them as I work!
- The more I work by hand, the more I learn: I find that the tools themselves teach me how to use them in the most effective way.
- My front porch shop annex has been a joy: It's truly been a pleasure to work there in the afternoon sunshine. I just bring up the components I'm working on, along with a small tote of hand tools, and I'm ready to go to work.

Perhaps the most significant, though subtle, change that has come out of my shift to hand tools is the sense of calm that I now feel while I do woodworking. It's not just the lack of noise or the absence of dust and danger; it's also due to the overall sense of not being in so much of a hurry anymore. Sure it takes me longer to build a piece of furniture with hand tools than it used to take when I worked with power tools in a production frame of mind. But the fact is I just don't care anymore! I'm never looking at the clock, anyway, as what I'm doing at the moment is just what I want to be doing every step of the way! The furniture that comes out at the end is just icing on the cake!

RESOURCES

FURTHER READING AND
VIDEOS IN THE USE OF
HANDTOOLS

Popular Woodworking Magazine
popularwoodworking.com

ShopWoodworking.com

RESOURCES

Adria Toolworks
604-710-5748
adriatools.com
Woodworking Tools

Anderson Planes
736-241-0138
andersonplanes.com
Woodworking Planes

Antique Used Tools
360) 452-2292
antique-used-tools.com
Vintage Hand Tools

Bench Crafted
benchcrafted.com
Workbench Hardware

Ron Brese Planes
706-647-8082
breseplane.com
Woodworking Planes

Bridge City Tools
800-253-3332
bridgecitytools.com
Woodworking Hand Tools

Di Legno Woodshop Supply
877-208-4298
dlws.com
Mallets, Marking gauges, Knives

E.C. Emmerich Planes
800-724-7758
ecemmerich.com
Woodworking Planes

Hock Tools
888-282-5233
hocktools.com
Woodworking Blades & Tools

Lee Valley Tools, LTD.
800-871-8158 (U.S.)
800-267-8767 (Canada)
leevalley.com
Woodworking Tools

Lie-Nielsen Toolworks
800-327-2520
lie-nielsen.com
Woodworking Tools

McFeeley's
519-733-0416
mcfeelys.com
Woodworking Screws

Medallion Toolworks
905-465-3799
medalliontoolworks.com
Custom Hand Saws

Old Street Tool, Inc.
479-981-3688
planemaker.com
Woodworking Planes

Ontario Adhesives
519-733-0416
ontarioadhesives.ca
Super-Phatic Glue

Rockler Woodworking
800-279-4441
rockler.com
Woodworking Tools

Stanley Tools
800-262-2161
stanleytools.com
Woodworking Tools

Jim Tolpin
jimtolpin.com
View Jim's portfolio, including his work on gypsy caravans, learn about his woodworking classes. You can also find insturctions on making more hand tool fixtures, including a multi-jig that converts any sturdy table into a planing bench.

Tremont Nail Company
800-835-0121
tremontnail.com
Cut Nails

Tools for Working Wood
800-426-4613
toolsforworkingwood.com
Woodworking Tools

Vintage Saws
vintagesaws.com
Vintage Hand Tools

Wenzloff & Sons
503-359-5255
wenzloffandsones.com
Custom Hand Saws

Woodcraft Supply
800-535-4482
woodcraft.com
Woodworking Tools

Wooden Boat Foundation
360-385-3628
shop.woodenboat.org
Rose-head nails and Washers

IDEAS. INSTRUCTION. INSPIRATION.

These and other great **Popular Woodworking** products are available at your local bookstore, woodworking store or online supplier.

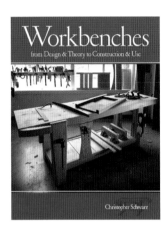

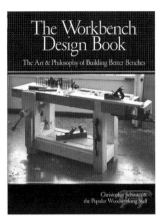

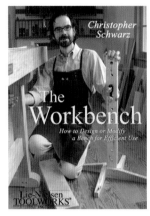

THE TABLE BOOK
BY CHRISTOPHER SCHWARZ
Workbenches uses historical records of the 18th and 19th centuries and breathes new life into traditional bench designs that are simpler than modern benches, easier to build and perfect for both power and hand tools.
ISBN 13: 978-1-55870-840-2
hardcover • 144 pages • Z1981

THE WORKBENCH DESIGN BOOK
BY CHRISTOPHER SCHWARZ
Which workbench should you build? This book explores centuries of workbench history to separate the enduring bench designs from the bad ones. Includes nine plans for shop-tested workbenches and makeovers of 10 other bench designs.The latest information on vises and other bench hardware.
ISBN 13: 978-1-4403-1040-9
hardcover• 144 pages • Y1532

POPULAR WOODWORKING MAGAZINE
Whether learning a new hobby or perfecting your craft, *Popular Woodworking Magazine* has expert information to teach the skill, not just the project. Find the latest issue on newsstands, or order online at www.popularwoodworking.com.

THE WORKBENCH DVD
BY CHRISTOPHER SCHWARZ
Chris Schwarz demonstrates various strategies for holding the workpiece for essential tasks, by designing or modifying a workbench for efficient use.
40 Minutes, DVD. Lie-Nielsen Toolworks Productions, 2008

 Purchase online at shopwoodworking.com
DVD • Z9818

Visit **www.popularwoodworking.com** to see more woodworking information by the experts.

Recent Articles	Featured Product	Note from the Editor
Read the five most recent articles from Popular Woodworking Books. • **Kitchen Makeovers - Pull-Out Pantry Design & Construction** • **Woodshop Lust Tom Rosati's Woodshop** • **Woodshop Lust David Thiel's Woodshop** • **Wood Finishing Simplified Strictly, Stickley Oak** • **Wood Finishing Simplified In a Pickle (Whitewash on Oak or Pine)**	**Made By Hand** $21.95 *Made By Hand* takes you right to the bench and shows you how to start building furniture using hand tools. By working through the six projects in this book, you'll learn the basics of hand-tool woodworking and how to use the tools effectively and efficiently, then add joinery skills and design complexity. The accompanying DVD includes valuable insight into the tools themselves and a look at the techniques that make these tools work so well.	**Welcome to Books & More** We've got the latest reviews and free sample excerpts from our favorite woodworking books, plus news on the newest releases. Check out the savings at our **Woodworker's Book Shop,** and don't miss out on building your Wish List for the holidays. If you missed our newsletter's **"Print Is Dead"** poll results, check them here, and subscribe (below) to our newsletter to receive special sale items and book reviews not found anywhere else. *– David Baker-Thiel, Executive Editor* *Popular Woodworking Books*

A woodworking education can come in many forms, including books, magazines, videos and community feedback. At Popular Woodworking we've got them all. Visit our website at www.popularwoodworking.com to follow our blogs, read about the newest tools and books and join our community. We want to know what you're building.

Sign up to receive our weekly newsletter at http://popularwoodworking.com/newsletters/